D0450266

CALIFORNIA

ART OF THE STATE

ART OF THE STATE

CALIFORNIA

The Spirit of America

Text by Nancy Friedman

Harry N. Abrams, Inc., Publishers

NEW YORK

This book was prepared for publication at
Walking Stick Press, San Francisco

Project staff:
Series Designer: Linda Herman
Series Editor: Diana Landau

For Harry N. Abrams, Inc.:
Series Editor: Ruth A. Peltason

Page 1: *You Are the Star,* mural by Thomas Suriya, corner of Hollywood and Wilcox, Los Angeles, 1983. *Photo Robert Holmes*

Page 2: *Cypress Trees—17 Mile Drive* by Mary DeNeale Morgan, c. 1925. *Trotter Galleries*

Library of Congress Cataloging-in-Publication Data

Friedman, Nancy.
California : the spirit of America state by state / by Nancy Friedman
p. cm. — (Art of the state)
ISBN 0-8109-5552-0 (hc)
1. California—Civilization—Pictorial works. I. Title.
II. Series.
F862.F75 1998
979.4—dc21 97-12016

Published in 1998 by Harry N. Abrams, Incorporated, New York

Printed and bound in the United States of America

Harry N. Abrams, Inc.
100 Fifth Avenue
New York, N.Y. 10011
www.abramsbooks.com

Stairway by James Doolin, 1991–92. *Koplin Gallery, Santa Monica*

CONTENTS

JAZZ
WEST
COAST
VOL. 3

"California is not so much a state of the Union as it is an imagi-nation...."

William Irwin Thompson

California is America's land of big dreams, the El Dorado at the continent's edge. From the days of European discovery to the present, it has been portrayed as a paradise of possibility and transformation, a place to make a "fresh start"—in the gold fields, the vineyards, the studio lots—and break free from bad weather, bad reputations, and social and economic oppression. The call was irresistible and universal. As a result, in a nation drawn from diverse cultures, California may be the most culturally diverse of all, claiming not only European, Native, and Pan-American roots but close ties to the Far East as well.

Even before the tides of immigration that helped shape California's last two centuries, this was a place of stunning variety and contradiction. In fact, it's been observed more than a few times that, geographically speaking, California is not one state but many: dry and wet, mountainous and flat, densely populated and virtually empty. The highest point in the Lower 48—Mount Whitney, at 14,495 feet above sea level—and the lowest point on the continent—Death Valley, at 282 feet below sea level—are a mere 85 miles apart. The state's 1,110 miles of coastline include broad swimming beaches and windswept, rock-strewn palisades. Lush orchards, ancient redwoods, palm oases, and desert sagebrush all coexist within California's six life zones, from Lower Sonoran to Alpine.

As a Spanish colony, California was two provinces: Alta (upper) and Baja (lower). Today, with Baja California attached to Mexico, a lingering

Spring Eternal by Langdon Smith, c. 1920. This image appeared on the cover of a booklet issued by the Orange County Chamber of Commerce. *Anaheim Public Library*

historical schism separates northern California from southern. When Los Angeles was still a sleepy Mexican village, San Francisco was a sophisticated, bustling metropolis; by the late 20th century they had switched roles. Los Angeles was a world-class megalopolis with a population of three and a half million and an area of 465 square miles, far outstripping San Francisco, which in recent times has traded heavily on its quaintness and tourist appeal. Deep political and cultural antagonisms continue to define and divide north and south. Not least of these is a nearly century-old struggle over control of the state's precious water, which tends to pit recreation- and conservation-minded northern Californians against development and agribusiness interests in the south state and Central Valley.

Still, to an outsider, the unifying themes stand out. Compared even with other Western states, California represents an optimistic face toward the future—the place where trends first get sampled and prepared for worldwide dissemination via the state's well-tooled entertainment industry. California's arts, commerce, and culture all reflect this spirit of aspiration, innovation, and redemption. From Albert Bierstadt's 19th-century landscapes to the Beach Boys' mid-20th-century surfer ballads, from Joaquin Miller's rapturous nature poetry to Disneyland's fantasy reinventions of Main Street and the Wild West, from Theosophy to est and the Crystal Cathedral, California has always surged with buoyant hopefulness—sometimes naive, sometimes prophetic.

But sunny optimism is only one of California's themes. Another current is dark and dramatic: mining claims that don't pan out, earthquakes that mock the permanence of human endeavor, economic booms that go bust. During the latter half of the 20th century, many artists and writers have explored

Napa Valley vineyard. *Photo Bruce McNitt/Panoramic Images*

this dark side of the California dream, exposing the shadows behind the sunshine. At the turn of the millennium, the arts often look critically, comically, or wryly at the dreamers and the objects of their dreams.

Still, for any number of reasons, California dreaming persists. However many hopes are dashed, the sense of possibility remains strong for each new generation, each new immigrant group that reaches California soil. "Were one to seek a working definition of the California Dream," suggests historian Kevin Starr, "it might be this: that because of a place called California, life might be better."

Perhaps it's something about the brilliant and persistent sunlight, the brisk westerly winds, the still-expansive landscapes and natural resources, the tension of North America meeting the Pacific along that great verge of coast. Of all the states in the Union, only California takes its name from fiction and its identity from dreams. But the real, tangible California with its diverse geography and weather and politics is even more interesting. The art of the state nurtures the dream, proclaims the reality, and—at its most successful—builds a bridge between them.✸

CALIFORNIA

"The Golden State"
31st State

Date of Statehood
SEPTEMBER 9, 1850

Capital
SACRAMENTO

Bird
VALLEY QUAIL

Flower
CALIFORNIA POPPY

Tree
REDWOOD

Mineral
NATIVE GOLD

Animal
CALIFORNIA GRIZZLY BEAR

Fish
GOLDEN TROUT

If you didn't already know California as a place of mingled fantasy and reality, a glance at the official list would offer some broad hints. "Eureka"—the only state motto in Greek—embodies the genius loci of ambiguous optimism. ("I have found"...what? Fame, fortune, enlightenment...or just the freeway?) The Great Seal of the state also features Minerva, the goddess who sprang full-grown from Jupiter's head—a symbol of California's tendency to reinvent itself at will. At her feet are a grizzly bear (alas, long extinct in the state) and a cluster of grapes, standing for wildlife and agricultural bounty. Both the bear and California's signature tree, the redwood, personify power, myth, and larger-than-life drama. The state bird, a perky quail, might have been imagined by a Disney

Valley quail and California poppy

Gold nugget

"Eureka" (I have found it)

State motto

animator. And then there is the official song: despite near-universal preference for the better-known "California, Here I Come," legislators in 1951 adopted "I Love You, California," which boasts the political virtues of praising all and offending no one.✸

Above: U.S. postage stamp marking the 1948 centennial of the Gold Rush. *Stamp King. Right:* Coast redwoods (*Sequoia sempervirens*) include some of the oldest and tallest trees on Earth. *Illustration by John Dawson, National Park Service. Left:* California's state seal rendered in stained glass, 1908. Designed by Albert Sutton and Charles Weeks, built by United Glass Works, San Francisco. The bear at Minerva's side underwent revision over the years before settling into its current alert posture. *State Capitol Bookstore*

Hang Town Fry

The great California food scribe M. F. K. Fisher recalls a San Francisco literary Bohemian (unnamed) waxing rhapsodic over this simple dish, which harks from the Gold Rush camps: "What about Hang Town Fry?...Why, it's the best food that ever sat before misbegotten man!" Fisher quotes this version, adapted from an early *Sunset Cook Book*:

2 dozen medium-sized California oysters
5 or 6 whole eggs
Fine white breadcrumbs
Melted butter

Drain and pat oysters dry, season with salt and pepper. Roll first in flour, then in beaten egg, then in breadcrumbs. Fry in melted butter until golden brown on one side; before turning them, pour over all 4 or 5 eggs beaten light. Let cook a minute, then turn and brown on other side to desired color. The Fry will look like an egg pancake with oysters mixed in.

Oakland librarian Ina Coolbrith was Jack London's chief mentor and co-founder with Bret Harte of *The Overland Monthly,* which published important California writers. She later became California's perpetual poet laureate. ***Bancroft Library***

Whence "California"?

The first use of the name "California" is found in the romantic novel *Las Sergas de Esplandián (The Deeds of Esplandián)* by Garcia Ordoñez de Montalvo, published in Spain in 1510. According to Montalvo, the fabulous island was ruled by Queen Calafia: "Know ye that at the right hand of the indies there is an island called California, very close to that part of the Terrestrial Paradise, which was inhabited by black women without a single man among them, and they lived in the manner of Amazons. They were robust of body with strong passionate hearts and great virtue. The island itself is one of the wildest in the world on account of the bold and craggy rocks."

The State Capitol in Sacramento, by architects Minor Frederick Butler and Reuben Clark, was completed in 1874. ***Photo Bill Ross***

"I Love You, California"

I love you, California, you're the greatest state of all....
Where the snow-crowned Golden Sierras
Keep their watch o'er the valley's bloom,
It is there I would be in our land by the sea,
Every breeze bearing rich perfume.
It is here nature gives of her rarest.
It is Home Sweet Home to me,
And I know when I die I shall breathe my last sigh
For my sunny California.

F. B. Silverwood and A. F. Frankenstein, 1913

"I Love You, California" was introduced in 1913 by operatic diva Mary Garden, who wrote to its composer: "I am proud indeed to be the first to sing your most beautiful song in public." *Sheet music courtesy Oakland Public Library*

Above: Of California's "official" creatures, four are endangered, including the dog-faced butterfly (*Zerene eurydice*). The desert tortoise, golden trout, and grizzly bear are also on the endangered list. *Photo Kjell B. Sandved/ Photo Researchers. Right:* California was briefly declared a republic when a band of American settlers rebelled against Spanish rule in 1846 under a grizzly bear flag designed by William B. Ide. *California State Library*

CALIFORNIA MILESTONES

1510 First mention of a place called "California," in novel *Las Sergas de Esplandián.*

1542 Juan Rodriguez Cabrillo sails into San Diego Harbor.

1579 Sir Francis Drake sails into Drakes Bay (Point Reyes).

1628 First published account of California in English: *The World Encompassed by Sir Francis Drake.*

1769 First permanent Spanish colony in California at San Diego.

1775 Monterey becomes capital of California.

1776 San Francisco founded.

1781 Los Angeles founded.

1810 Mexican rebellion against Spain begins.

1821 Spain grants independence to Mexico.

1831–36 "Californios" revolt against the Mexican government.

1841 First American wagon train arrives in California.

1846 Bear Flag of "California Republic" raised; independence lasts three weeks.

1846–47 Donner Party trapped in Sierra Nevada snows.

1847 American victory at battle of La Mesa ends war with Californios. Non-Indian population is 15,000.

1848 James Marshall discovers gold at Sutter's Mill.

1849 Gold seekers flock to California. Statehood movement begins; capital moves to San Jose.

1850 California becomes 31st state. Population 93,000.

1854 Sacramento becomes state capital.

1863 Painter Albert Bierstadt first visits California.

1868 Bret Harte and Ina Coolbrith found *The Overland Monthly.*

1869 Transcontinental railroad completed.

1870 Population 560,247.

1873 California's last Indian conflict, the Modoc War, ends.

1884 Publication of *Ramona,* by Helen Hunt Jackson.

1885 First trainload of southern California oranges reaches eastern markets.

1890 Yosemite and Sequoia National Parks founded. Population 1,213,398.

1901 Frank Norris publishes *The Octopus.*

1903 Carmel-by-the-Sea established as an artists' colony.

1906 San Francisco earthquake and fire.

1908 First motion picture is made in Los Angeles.

1913 Los Angeles Museum of History, Science and Art holds its first exhibition in Exposition Park.

1915 Panama-Pacific Exposition held in San Francisco; Panama-California International Exposition held in San Diego.

1919 Hearst Castle completed.

1921-54 Construction of Watts Towers (never completed).

1927 Philo Farnsworth transmits first television picture from San Francisco.

1930 State population is 5,677,102. Los Angeles population is 1.2 million.

1932 Summer Olympic Games held in Los Angeles. Group f.64 formed in Oakland by Ansel Adams, Imogen Cunningham, and others.

1937 Golden Gate Bridge opens.

1939 Golden Gate International Exposition held on Treasure Island, San Francisco. John Steinbeck publishes *The Grapes of Wrath*.

1942 President Roosevelt orders internment of Japanese-Americans in California.

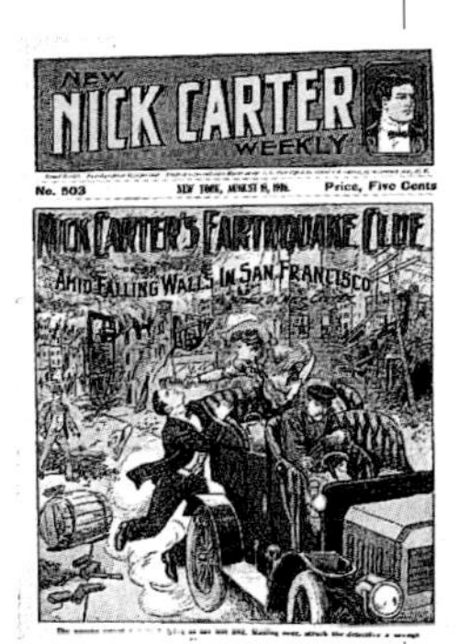

1945 United Nations founded in San Francisco.

1950 Richard Nixon elected to U.S. Senate. Population 10.6 million.

1957 Brooklyn Dodgers move to Los Angeles; New York Giants move to San Francisco.

1960 Winter Olympic Games held in Squaw Valley.

1962 With 16 million residents, California becomes the nation's most populous state.

1964 Free Speech Movement begins on the U.C. Berkeley campus.

1965 Watts riots erupt in Los Angeles.

1984 Summer Olympic Games held in Los Angeles.

1989 Loma Prieta earthquake (San Francisco Bay Area).

1994 Northridge earthquake (Los Angeles). Population 32 million.

1998–2000 Sesquicentennial of gold discovery through statehood.

California's diversity begins with its landscape, which is literally transcontinental in scope. The Siskiyou Mountains of the north are part of the Cascade range that begins in British Columbia; the peninsular range, from Mount San Jacinto south, extends into Mexico. Active volcanoes simmer in the northeast; prehistoric tar pits bubble in the heart of Los Angeles. Average annual rainfall in parts of the north approaches 100 inches; on the floor of Death Valley, it is less than 2 inches. Some places along the coast could be mistaken for Maine, or Genoa, or Waikiki; other places in California's deserts and high mountains are as bleak and eerie as the surface of the moon. Grass-

California as El Dorado: gently rolling hillsides carpeted with golden flowers and glowing in the benign, ever-present sunshine. *Above:* Portrait of the state flower, the California poppy (*Eschscholtzia californica*). *Photo Barbara Gerlach. Right: Silver and Gold* by Granville Redmond, c. 1918. *Orange County Museum of Art*

land and farmland, rainforest and dry waste—California geography is a world unto itself. And when you think you've grasped its complexity, along comes an earthquake to unsettle the land—and your assumptions. ✸

California as wilderness: desolate, rock-strewn high country in the Sierra. *Above: Mount Williamson, the Sierra Nevada, from Manzanar, California* by Ansel Adams, 1945. © *Ansel Adams Publishing Rights Trust*

"IN CALIFORNIA, UNLESS YOU ARE AFRAID OF THE RAIN, NATURE welcomes you at almost any time. The union of the man and the visible universe is free, is entirely unchecked by any hostility on the part of nature...."

Josiah Royce, 1898

Harvest Time by William Hahn, 1875. California's Central Valley was a vast inland sea in prehistoric times. Mineral deposits made the soil a paradise of fertility, as evidenced in this early scene of a wheat harvest. *Fine Arts Museums of San Francisco*

Mountain and Valley

The Spanish missionaries, journeying north from Mexico, barely noted California's fortresslike mountains. Later pioneers, coming from the eastern United States, had a different perspective. The Sierra Nevada is an intimidating barrier of granite running half the state's length. Its eastern slope looks like a 2-mile-high wall, and it is only *one* of California's many mountain ranges. On the west, the relatively gentle Coast Ranges extend from the far northwest almost to Los Angeles. The east-west Cascade and Klamath ranges define the northern border; the Tehachapis stand sentry over the south, while the rugged San Gabriel and San Bernardino Mountains bisect it. Nestled between the ranges are valleys of every size and description, from raw and remote to—in the case of the great Central Valley—incomparably rich and fertile.

"BUT OUR GRANDEST VIEW WAS EASTWARD, ABOVE THE DEEP sheltered valley and over the tops of those terrible granite walls, out upon rolling ridges of stone and wonderful granite domes. Nothing in the whole list of irruptive products, except volcanoes themselves, is so wonderful as these domed mountains. They are of every variety of conoidal form, having... profiles varying from such semicircles as the cap behind the Sentinel to the graceful infinite curves of the North Dome. Above and beyond these stretch back long bare ridges connecting with sunny summit peaks."

Clarence King, Mountaineering in the Sierra Nevada, *1872*

Southern Sierras **by Joseph Breuer, 1915. Literally "snowy mountain range," the Sierra Nevada was formed from a single block of granite and includes the highest point in the Lower 48, Mount Whitney.** ***Courtesy Joseph Szymanski***

INCOMPARABLE YOSEMITE

To most people, Yosemite *is* its valley—that vale of awe carved by glaciers and wind into a cathedral of sculpted granite walls laced with bright waterfalls. But the surrounding park spans nearly three-quarter-million acres of rugged peaks, forests, and meadows. Miwok Indians inhabited the region for centuries before white explorers first beheld its wonders in 1851. Just a few decades later, thanks largely to the work of naturalist John Muir, it was designated as our second national park, in time to forestall the depredations of grazing and logging. Today Yosemite is threatened only by being loved too much. ✹

"HERE THE VIEW IS PERFECTLY FREE DOWN INTO THE HEART OF THE BRIGHT IRISED throng of comet-like streamers into which the whole volume of the fall separates, two or three hundred feet below the brow. So glorious a display of pure wildness, acting at close range while cut off from all the world beside, is terribly impressive . . . the huge steadfast rocks, the flying waters, and the rainbow light forming one of the most glorious pictures conceivable."

John Muir, The Yosemite, *1912*

Left: Bridal Veil Falls, Yosemite, by Albert Bierstadt, c. 1871–73. The artist made his reputation on his meticulously rendered views of Yosemite Valley, composed in his New York studio from sketches made in the field. Upon first visiting the valley, he wrote: "We are now here in the Garden of Eden. . . ." *North Carolina Museum of Art. Opposite:* John Muir, photographed in Yosemite during a Sierra Club outing in 1907 or 1908. Muir, who lived in the valley for many years, was instrumental not only in founding the national park but in deciphering the origins of Yosemite's dramatic landforms. *Bancroft Library. Opposite below:* Yellow-bellied marmot, a familiar denizen of the Sierra Nevada, by John James Audubon and John Woodhouse Audubon

Dunes, palm trees, and prospectors evoke the archetypal California desert. *Right:* 1920s brochure for a Death Valley resort. *Below:* *Palm Tree, California* by Richard Misrach, 1975. *Courtesy of the artist.* *Opposite: Death Valley, Dante's View* by Fernand Lungren, c. 1900–1925. *University Art Museum, Santa Barbara*

California's three deserts—the Great Basin Desert in the north, the Colorado in the south, and the Mojave in the middle—are together about the size of Ohio. They comprise the affluent (and assiduously irrigated) oasis of Palm Springs, the ghost town of Bodie, military bases and testing grounds, lush date palms and stark Joshua trees, and an awesome assortment of sand dunes, mountains, badlands, arroyos, and dry lakebeds.✸

"THE NATURAL CONDITION OF humankind in this landscape is one of dauntedness. To define the scenery as 'breathtaking' doesn't explain exactly how it takes away your breath: by sitting on your chest and pressing on your head... in its enormity, it constantly challenges you to comprehend it, to come to terms with infinity."

David Darlington, The Mojave, *1996*

"EAST AWAY FROM THE SIERRAS, SOUTH from Panamint and Amargosa, east and south many an uncounted mile, is the Country of Lost Borders. Ute, Paiute, Mojave, and Shoshone inhabit its frontiers, and as far into the heart of it as a man dare go. Not the law, but the land sets the limit. Desert is the name it wears upon the maps, but the Indian's is the better word. Desert is a loose term to indicate land that supports no man; whether the land can be bitted and broken to that purpose is not proven. Void of life it never is, however dry the air and villainous the soil."

Mary Austin, The Land of Little Rain, *1903*

Going to Extremes

HIGH TEMPERATURE
134°F (Death Valley, July 10, 1913)

LOW TEMPERATURE
-45°F (Boca Reservoir, Nevada County, Jan. 20, 1937)

MOST PRECIPITATION, ONE SEASONAL YEAR
254.9" (Camp Six, Del Norte County, 1981–82)

LEAST PRECIPITATION, ONE CALENDAR YEAR
0 inches (Death Valley, 1929; Baghdad, San Bernardino County, 1913)

SNOWFALL, ONE STORM
189" (Mount Shasta, Feb. 13–19, 1959)

SNOW DEPTH
451" (Alpine County, Mar. 11, 1911)

WIND SPEED
101 mph gust (Sanburg, L.A. County, Mar. 25, 1975)

Sea Otters

From the beaches of Santa Cruz, Monterey, and San Luis Obispo counties, the lucky visitor can glimpse southern sea otters *(Enhydra lutris nereis)* floating on their backs amid the kelp beds. These charming marine mammals are primatelike in their use of tools: carrying rocks in their paws, they pry shellfish from the sea bottom, then hammer the shells open on their chests. Between 1741 and 1911, fur traders hunted sea otters nearly to extinction; today the animals are protected by state and federal laws.

Up and Down the Coast

"The Coast" is Eastern shorthand for California; in the popular imagination, the coastal fringe *is* California, a Shangri-la of sandy beaches and waving palms, suntanned surfers and bikinied starlets. In reality, the coast—all 1,100 miles of it—is even more wondrous and varied. In Del Norte and Humboldt counties, it is towering redwoods and miles of inaccessible "Lost Coast." In Big Sur, it is wind-warped Monterey cypresses and golden multitudes of Monarch butterflies. From Santa Barbara south, it is "surf turf" and oil derricks bobbing offshore like toy birds. More than 40 percent of California's shoreline is publicly owned and accessible—the greatest percentage of any coastal state.

Drawing by Paul Kratter, 1997. *Courtesy of the artist*

I gazing at the boundaries of granite and spray,

the established sea-marks, felt behind me
Mountain and plain, the immense breadth of the continent,
before me the mass and doubled stretch of water.

Robinson Jeffers, "Continent's End," 1924

Much of California's coast is rugged and unapproachable. *Opposite: Seal Rock* by Albert Bierstadt, c. 1872. *New Britain Museum of American Art. Photo Michael Agee. Above: Point Lobos* by Guy Rose, c. 1918. *The Irvine Museum*

Natural disasters in California tend toward the biblical. Seasonal wildfires ravage the dry landscape—not just in forests but in densely populated cities, as Malibu learned in 1993 and Oakland in 1991. Unaccustomed to much rainfall in a "normal" year, the earth responds to cyclical deluges with devastating floods. And the state is a chaos of seismic activity, the result of the subterranean clash of two tectonic plates: the San Andreas Fault system alone includes six minor fault zones continuously

bumping and grinding in their underground war dance. "For a single minute" after the 1989 San Francisco quake, writes Bill Barich, "we'd been liberated from our orderly illusions and subjected to the chaotic laws of nature, our lives tossed into the sky, and a new set of transformations was beginning."

"THE ENTIRE FRONT OF A FOUR-STORY BRICK BUILDING IN THIRD STREET sprung outward like a door and fell sprawling across the street, raising a dust like a great volume of smoke! And here came the buggy—overboard went the man, and in less time than I can tell it the vehicle was distributed in small fragments along three hundred yards of the street."

Mark Twain, Roughing It, *1863*

California's character has been shaped by fire, flood, earthquake, and drought. *Above: San Francisco Fire* by William A. Coulter, 1906. *Hirschl & Adler Galleries, New York* *Opposite below: Sunset* magazine cover depicting a vision of a glorious new city arising from the rubble of the great quake. *Lane Publications* *Right:* An artist sketches in the ruins of the Palace of Fine Arts after the 1906 quake. *California Historical Society*

19th-century lithograph of Northern Valley Yokut hunters stalking game, from an 1816 watercolor by Louis Choris. *Bancroft Library. Below:* Carved elk antler purse, used by the Klamath tribe to carry shells for trading purposes. *Oakland Museum*

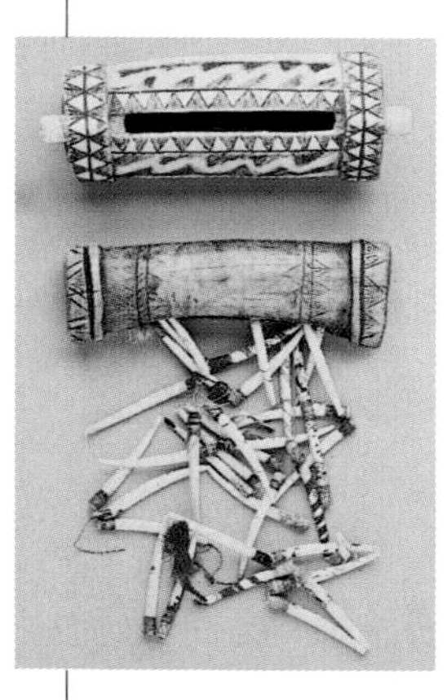

In 1579, when Sir Francis Drake sailed into what is now Point Reyes, the aboriginal Californians were one of the most diverse populations on the planet. Scattered in small settlements from Humboldt Bay on the north coast to the Mojave Desert in the southeast, they spoke more than 100 dialects of 21 language families. Rugged mountains, rivers, and deserts kept populations isolated. Yet thanks to the benign climate and the virtual absence of warfare, California was home to a quarter-million natives, from the Klamath and Hupa in the far north to the Yangna of the Los Angeles Basin to the Mojave and Yuma in the southeast.

Despite their linguistic differences, many natives shared a similar lifestyle. They lived in round or conical huts made of indigenous materials and made acorn meal from the fruit of California's abundant oaks. Villages commonly were no larger than 250 people. Only the southeastern peoples made pottery; elsewhere, intricately woven baskets were used for gathering and winnowing grain, storing water, and—with the addition of hot stones—cooking food. The food was everywhere plentiful: salmon in the rivers; shellfish on the coast; bear, elk, and deer in the valleys and foothills. ✸

Twined or coiled baskets were made by the women of every California tribe. *Above:* Annie Burke, Pomo basketweaver. *California State Library* *Left:* Paiute Panamint-style basket by Rosie Noble (Panamint Shoshone), c. pre-1915. *San Diego Museum of Man. Photo Ken Hedges*

"THE HEATHEN SEEM TO BE VERY WELL SUPPLIED WITH everything, especially with plenty of fish of all kinds; in fact they brought to the camp so much that it was necessary to tell them not to bring any more, for it would eventually have to spoil."

Fray Crespi, encamped near Santa Barbara, August 1769

Acorn Mush

When the acorn crop was ripe in the fall, entire villages turned out to gather and store the nuts for their year's supply. Acorns were shelled and ground by hand on a flat stone into a coarse meal or flour, which was leached of its poisonous tannic acid by spreading it into a pit of sand by a stream, or in a large bowl. Letting the sand settle, the women then scooped off the clean meal. Mush was cooked in a basket by adding hot stones to a mixture of meal and water.

Artists in Stone and Wood

The most accomplished artisans of pre-European California were surely the Chumash, who lived between present-day Ventura and Point Conception. Their 30-foot-long seagoing canoes, unique in North America, were crafted of driftwood, stitched with deer sinew, and daubed with asphaltum for watertightness. Using flint knives, they carved beautifully detailed bowls of wood and soapstone. Their dome houses, up to 60 feet in diameter, sheltered three or four families each. Their most dazzling accomplishment may have been their abstract paintings on rock walls, the work of cult members who believed the pictographs bonded them to their mystic past. As late as 1870, Chumash Indians, headed by the chieftainess Pomposa, were living near Saticoy Springs.

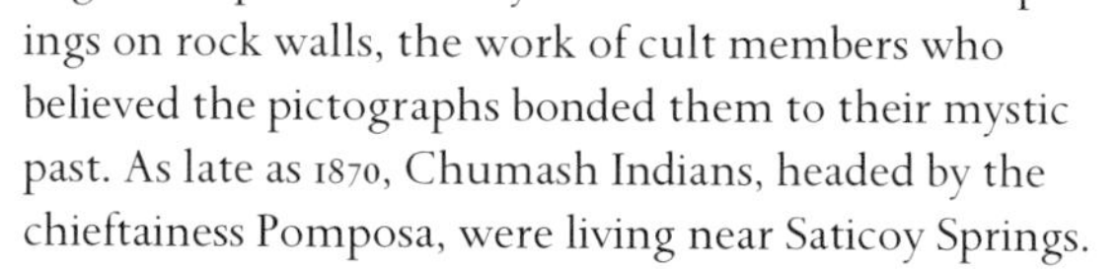

The acorn was truly the "staff of life" for native people throughout California. *Left:* Indian Grinding Rocks State Historic Park, near Highway 49. *Photo Robert Holmes* *Above:* Coso Range petroglyph featuring a decorated human figure with a lizard dangling from its right arm. *Photo Fred Hirschmann.* *Opposite:* Ishi, the last "wild Indian" of North America, demonstrating bowmaking. Photo by A. L. Kroeber, 1914. *Phoebe Hearst Museum of Anthropology, University of California, Berkeley*

In the land of Dreams

Find your Grown-up Self
Your future Family.

Wintu song

The Last "Wild Indian"

"This man is undoubtedly wild. He has pieces of deer thong in place of ornaments in the lobes of his ears and a wooden plug in the septum of his nose. He recognizes most of my Yana words and a fair proportion of his own seem to be identical [with mine]. . . . If I am not mistaken, he's full of religion—bathing at sunrise, putting out pinches of tobacco where the lightning strikes, etc. . . . We showed him some arrows last night, and we could hardly get them away from him. He showed us how he flaked the points, singed the edges of the feathering, and put on the sinew wrappings."

From a letter by University of California anthropologist T. T. Waterman describing Ishi, the last "wild Indian" of North America, discovered at a corral near Oroville in August 1911

Flower Dance Spirit by Frank LaPena, 1981. LaPena was born in San Francisco to Wintu-Nomtipom and Asian parents. Among the Wintu people of northern California, the spring Flower Dance celebrates renewal and is a time of healing, forgiveness, and blessings. *Courtesy of the artist*

EXPLORING "ALTA CALIFORNIA"

Mid-18th-century maps still depicted California as an island. ***Bancroft Library***

Joao Rodriguez Cabrilho (or Cabrillo), a Portuguese navigator for the Spanish, was the first European to reach Alta (upper) California. His 1542–43 trip was cut short, and for decades the Spaniards concentrated on their more profitable lands to the south. Meanwhile, Sir Francis Drake arrived via the Strait of Magellan at a bay north of San Francisco. Drake and his crew spent a month there in 1579 repairing their ship, the *Golden Hind,* and miscommunicating with natives. Drake then returned to preying on Spanish treasure ships in the Pacific; otherwise California might today be called "New Albion," the name Drake gave it for the glory of Elizabeth I.

In 1702, Eusebio Francisco Kino, exploring down the Colorado River for New Spain, realized that, contrary to his maps, California was not an island. With overland exploration feasible, an expedition marched from Mexico City to San Diego in 1768. A Franciscan, Junipero Serra, began establishing Catholic missions along El Camino Real, a 600-mile route from San Diego to Sonoma. The 21 missions, all a day's walk apart, became settlement hubs and sites for converting local Indians to *gente de razón* ("people of reason").✸

"[THE MISSIONS] WERE LIKE PALACES...THERE WERE thousands of Indians in every one of them; thousands and thousands, all working so happy and peaceful."

A naive (at best) view of mission life from Helen Hunt Jackson's novel Ramona, *1884*

Opposite: **Spanish armor, late 17th century.** ***Oakland Museum. Above: Mission San Gabriel*** **by Ferdinand Deppe, 1832.** ***Santa Barbara Mission Archive Library***

Right: **The plate left in Drakes Bay by Sir Francis Drake's party in 1579. It was discovered more than three centuries later.** ***Bancroft Library***

Taking of Monterey by William Henry Meyers, 1842—a patriotic Yankee watercolor complete with musical accompaniment. The U.S. Marines seized the undefended fort, then retreated discreetly when they found no evidence that the U.S. and Mexico were at war. *Bancroft Library*
Below: Illustration by N. C. Wyeth from a 1939 edition of *Ramona.*
Opposite: Californians Catching Wild Horses with Riata by Hugo Wilhelm Arthur Nahl, c. 1866. *Oakland Museum*

The first Spanish colonists who were neither soldiers nor missionaries were lured to Alta California in the 1780s by reports of fat cattle herds and promises of generous land grants. By 1824, each *ranchero* was guaranteed 2,000 head of cattle and no taxes for five years. It was a relatively easy lifestyle that thrived after Mexico won independence from Spain in 1821. When the missions were secularized in 1834, the remaining Indians went to work on the *ranchos,* where in general they fared much better. Unlike the missionaries, who had cultivated grapes, figs, citrus fruit, and olives, the *rancheros* were interested in only one product: cattle—more specifically, cattle hides, in huge demand back East.✸

"AS LONG AS THERE WERE HIDES TO BE HAD, A MAN COULD BUY dazzling clothes for himself and his women, bedeck his horses with silver-mounted saddles and bridles. Since most of the inhabitants were unable to read or write, they felt no need for libraries. They sang endlessly to their guitars and did not miss concerts. They ate well, if simply, and were healthy."

David Lavender, California: Land of New Beginnings, *1972*

Cattle hides were known as "California dollars"; this branding iron makes the point graphically.

Los Angeles County Museum of Natural History

In January 1848, while building a sawmill at Sutter's Fort on the American River, a young wagon builder named James Wilson Marshall picked up a pea-size piece of yellow metal from the water. Within six months the news of his discovery had touched off a global frenzy: Gold Fever. Mining camps sprang up overnight; enterprising businessmen like Levi Strauss and entertainers like Lola Montez made fortunes catering to miners' needs. Between 1847 and statehood in 1850, California's population grew from 15,000 to 92,497; by 1860 it would reach nearly 380,000. Today, visitors can tour the Mother Lode country on State Highway 49, named for the Forty-Niners. Along its route are restored towns, spectacular caverns, abandoned mines, Victorian B&Bs, and opportunities to try panning for gold.✸

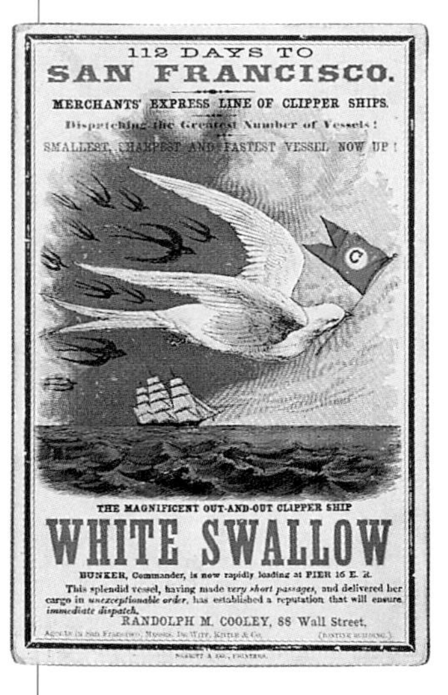

"THE BLACKSMITH DROPPED HIS HAMMER, THE carpenter his plane, the mason his trowel, the farmer his sickle, the baker his loaf, and the tapster his bottle. All were off for the mines, some on horses, some on carts, and some on crutches, and one went in a litter."

Walter Colton, Vermont native, Congregationalist clergyman, and alcalde *(judge) of Monterey from 1846–48*

Oh, what was your name in the States?

Was it Thompson or Johnson or Bates?
Did you murder your wife
And fly for your life?
Say, what was your name in the States?

California Gold Rush song

Miners in the Sierras by Charles Christian Nahl with Frederick A. Wenderoth, 1851–52. *National Museum of American Art/Art Resource* *Opposite above:* "Forty-Niners" such as the well-armed fellow in the framed portrait endured long sea journeys to reach the gold fields. *Bancroft Library. Opposite below:* Advertisement for a Clipper ship. *New-York Historical Society*

The Bonanza Kings

Gold brought the world to California; silver brought worldliness. Strictly speaking, the silver came not from California but from the eastern Sierra in neighboring Nevada; the discovery in 1859 of the Comstock Lode—a massive vein more than two miles long and a hundred feet wide—made millionaires and created a new social order headquartered in San Francisco. These "Bonanza Kings" built and decorated great mansions in San Francisco and Sacramento, commissioned portraits, endowed public buildings and institutions, and imported opera singers. Most prominent among them were the "Big Four"—Charles Crocker, Collis Huntington, Mark Hopkins, and Leland Stanford—financiers of the western end of the transcontinental railroad, whose construction brought thousands of immigrant Chinese laborers to California, and whose completion brought thousands more Easterners to the Golden State.

"Let out another link... *Work on as though Heaven was before you and Hell was behind you.*"

Collis Huntington, in a letter to Charles Crocker, 1866

The miners came in forty-nine/The whores in fifty-one;
When they got together/They produced the native son.

19th-century doggerel

Opposite above: Lola Montez, danseuse of the gold camps, in a Nathaniel Currier engraving. *Museum of the City of New York. Opposite below:* Tea urn made with Comstock Lode silver, 1860. *Oakland Museum. Above and top:* Mark Hopkins and his Nob Hill mansion, c. 1890. *Bancroft Library, California Historical Society. Right:* Levi Strauss first made blue jeans for the Forty-Niners and later begat one of San Francisco's first families.

"It is the chosen spot of all this earth...

as far as nature is concerned....I cannot describe it! I almost have to cry for joy when I look upon the lovely valley from the hillsides."

Luther Burbank, arriving in the Sonoma Valley in 1875

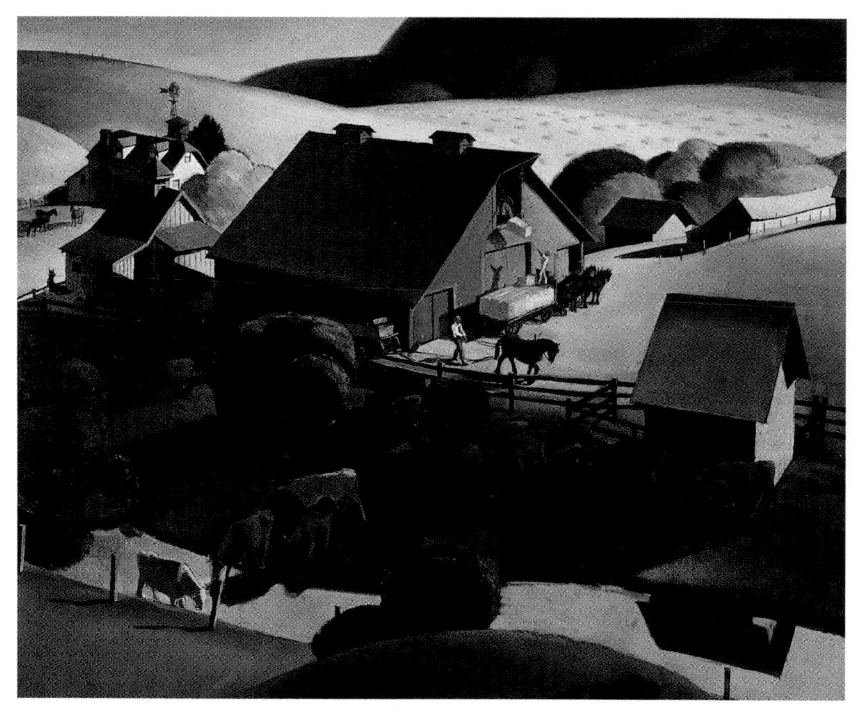

Ranch Near San Luis Obispo, Evening Light by Phil Paradise, 1935. *The Buck Collection*

The friars and *rancheros* who colonized Spanish California established the pattern for future California agribusiness. Bigger was better. The typical California farm is centrally controlled, and almost completely dependent on irrigation, machinery, and chemicals. Of those three elements, water has always been the most crucial. Irrigation turned the semi-arid Imperial Valley into the nation's "lettuce bowl" and made it possible to grow rice in Sacramento, which receives no rainfall in the summer at all. Irrigation enables California to be the nation's number one producer of cotton, grapes, wheat, and tree fruit such as plums and pears.✸

Above: **A complex irrigation system allows farmers, like this one in Stanislaus County, to flood their fields for rice growing. Photographer unknown.** ***California Historical Society***

Luther Burbank, Plant Man

Luther Burbank, who was directly or indirectly responsible for the dramatic growth of the state's fruit and vegetable industries in the late 19th century, arrived in California in 1875. Through his work with plant genetics he developed the Burbank potato, Burbank cherry, Burbank rose, Shasta daisy, 60 varieties of plums and prunes, 10 varieties of berries, and other fruits and vegetables. The Luther Burbank Gardens in Santa Rosa are open to the public daily.

Seed posters and crate labels promoted a cornucopian California, brimming with fresh produce year round. *Ferry-Morse Seed Company, California Historical Society*

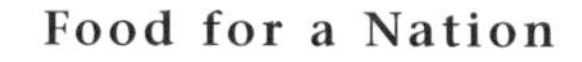

Food for a Nation

As the Gold Rush waned, land fever took its place. The first California land boom, in the late 1860s, saw the old land-grant *ranchos* divided into lots of 40 acres and up. By the 1870s, California was the second-largest wheat producer in the Union.

The Central Valley became a huge granary, and large-scale mechanization was first developed. But wheat profits suffered dramatically from the ruthlessness of the railroad barons, who charged exorbitant freight rates.

Come on down to Turlock,
We'll meet you at the train.
Look our district over,
You'll have everything to gain.
Here's where the crops are bumper,
You'll have to be a humper,
To keep in line with Turlock,
Where the watermelons grow.

Doggerel, c. 1915

Gold on the Trees

No California fruit has captured the national imagination as persistently and romantically as the orange. First planted from Old World stock by Franciscan missionaries, oranges became a commercial success after the introduction of a seedless Brazilian variety to Riverside County in 1873. The image of boughs heavy with golden fruit—all winter long!—played seductively to American fantasies of California, fantasies shamelessly encouraged in countless trademarks and picture postcards.

Still Life and Blossoming Almond Trees (The Stern Mural) by Diego Rivera, 1931. The great Mexican muralist created some of San Francisco's most striking public art, and influenced many local artists as well. *University of California, Berkeley. Left:* From a hand-tinted postcard by Edward Mitchell, San Francisco, 1909

From the Land to the Table

While California agribusiness seemed to grow ever bigger and its products ever blander, by the late 1970s a quiet countertrend was building. Inspired by the fresh seasonal foods she'd tasted in France, Alice Waters opened a small Berkeley restaurant, Chez Panisse, and began buying produce, meat, and cheese from tiny, quality-obsessed local suppliers. Across the bay in San Francisco, Frances Moore Lappé was finding willing ears for her message that simpler fare was healthier—for people and for the planet. By the 1980s it seemed you could scarcely twirl your fork without snagging a leaf of arugula, a slice of kiwi, or a morsel of California goat cheese.

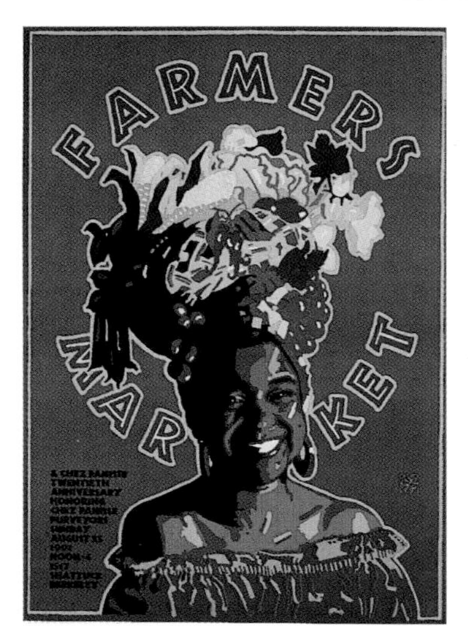

"IF, AS I BELIEVE, RESTAURANTS ARE COMMUNITIES—EACH with its own culture—then Chez Panisse began as a hunter-gatherer culture.... Not only did we prowl the supermarkets, the stores and stalls of Chinatown, and such speciality shops as Berkeley then possessed...we also literally foraged. We gathered watercress from streams, picked nasturtiums and fennel from roadsides, and gathered blackberries from the Santa Fe tracks.... We also took herbs from the gardens of friends."

Alice Waters, "The Farm–Restaurant Connection,"
Journal of Gastronomy, *1989*

Among the Vines

The missionaries planted vineyards from Mexican "criolla" grapes, to make sacramental wine and the brandy known as *aguardiente*. After secularization, the vineyards were mostly abandoned. It fell to an eccentric Hungarian nobleman, Agoston Haraszthy, to bring sophisticated cultivation, fermentation, and marketing techniques to California's wine industry. By 1857 Haraszthy had singlehandedly tripled the vineyard acreage in Sonoma Valley and introduced the distinctive Zinfandel grape, a variety whose origins are mysterious and whose wine became synonymous with California. By the 1960s, a new wave of gentleman (and lady) farmers were buying land in the valleys and producing wines that would eventually rival the great vintages of France.

Opposite above: Poster by David Lance Golnes, 1991. *Courtesy of the artist. Opposite below:* California cuisine as still life. *Photo Kathryn Kleinman. Above:* Cabernet Sauvignon grape cluster. *Photo Kerrick James. Left:* This was the Inglenook Vineyard circa 1920 and is today the Niebaum Coppola Estate Vineyards and Winery. *Courtesy of the winery*

Right: The Caspar by Herman R. Dietz, c. 1890. A steam schooner used mainly to transport lumber, the *Caspar* was built by Hanson and Frazer Shipyards in San Francisco. It was wrecked on the treacherous coast in 1897. *San Francisco Maritime NHP. Below:* The Carson Mansion in Eureka. The state's Victorian homes, big and small, were made possible by its bounteous timber harvest. *Photo Robert Holmes*

A State Built of Timber

California's redwood forests contain the world's oldest, largest, and tallest trees, and once virtually covered the state's northwest. Further inland, towering Douglas fir blanketed the Siskiyous.

Early settlers believed the trees to be an infinite resource, and logged accordingly. California's early trading and fishing fleet, the bridges and trestles that brought the railroad over the Sierra, and the post–Gold Rush mansions of Eureka, Sacramento, and San Francisco all owed their existence to the timber bounty. Logging continues to be important today, though in the last 150 years nearly 90 percent of the virgin forest has been destroyed: outside of protected areas, only about 5,000 acres of ancient forest remain in the state.

"IF YOU'VE SEEN ONE REDWOOD, YOU'VE SEEN THEM ALL."

Attributed to then-Governor Ronald Reagan at a 1966 press conference (and since denied)

Catch of the Day

California's early explorers told of salmon, sturgeon, and sardines so numerous they could practically be scooped out of streams and bays. As with most of the state's natural resources, abundance led to greed and depletion. Sturgeon are almost nonexistent; the golden trout (the state fish) is endangered; and the delectable Dungeness crab is only slowly making a comeback. Sport and commercial fishing remain popular, and aquaculture, notably oyster farming around Tomales Bay, has recently prospered.

Men of the Sea by Armin C. Hansen, 1920. Monterey Bay is in the background. Monterey's Cannery Row began as a fishing community of Chinese immigrants in the 1850s. The sardine catch peaked in 1941–42 at 250,287 tons. Reckless overfishing depleted supplies; fires destroyed the canneries. *Monterey Museum of Art*

"IN THE MORNING WHEN THE SARDINE FLEET HAS MADE A CATCH, the purse-seiners waddle heavily into the bay blowing their whistles. The deep-laden boats pull in against the coast where the canneries dip their tails into the bay. . . . Then cannery whistles scream and all over the town men and women scramble into their clothes and come running down to the Row to go to work."

John Steinbeck, Cannery Row, *1945*

ARTICLES OF FAITH

"And what is your religion?" I asked him.
"I think it is California," he replied.

From an interview with Swiss painter Gottardo Pazzoni, c. 1930s

California has beckoned not only those who sought to transform their material fate, but those seeking spiritual refuge or discovery. Both orthodox and unconventional religions have flourished throughout the state's history, along with a strong pantheistic streak—not surprising in a place of astonishing natural wonders. The pattern was set by the Natives: the World Renewal Indians, for example, believed that natural disasters—fires, earthquakes, lightning—were caused by supernatural forces; ceremonies helped keep those forces in check. For later settlers, from Franciscan friars to freethinkers like John Muir, Nature represented, even substituted for, the Creator.

Protestant ministers descended on California to save souls from Catholicism—dominant since mission days—and the godlessness of the mining camps. But California's religious diversity truly flowered in the 20th century, beginning with a maverick preacher named Aimee Semple McPherson, who

literally descended on San Diego in 1918, scattering tracts from an airplane. Her Four Square Gospel Church is still going strong. Spiritual leaders of all stripes have flourished here, from the Episcopal Bishop James Pike, who oversaw the building of San Francisco's Grace Cathedral and later vanished into the Jordanian desert, to Robert Schuller with his Crystal Cathedral and "Hour of Power" TV ministry. Eastern metaphysics, from Theosophy to Krishnamurti to Zen Buddhism and still more exotic strains, also have found a receptive home.✸

Opposite above: Four Square Gospel tambourine. *Oakland Museum* *Opposite below:* Theosophical Society program. *San Diego Historical Society* *Left:* Interior of Crystal Cathedral, designed by Philip Johnson. *Photo Robert Holmes.* *Below:* *Star Gazer* by Agnes Pelton, 1929. She often painted from metaphysical themes. *Private collection*

"HE VISITED THE 'CHURCH OF CHRIST, PHYSICAL,' WHERE holiness was attained through the constant use of chest-weights and spring grips; the 'Church Invisible' where fortunes were told and the dead made to find lost objects; the 'Tabernacle of the Third Coming,' where a woman in male clothing preached the 'Crusade Against Salt'; and the 'Temple Modern' under whose glass and chromium roof 'Brain-Breathing,' the Secret of the Aztecs, was taught."

Nathanael West, The Day of the Locust, *1933*

"I am not a member of any organized political party. I am a California Democrat."

Will Rogers

Emperor Norton
Joshua Norton, an English Jew, came to San Francisco in 1849, made and lost a fortune, and disappeared for a few years. He resurfaced with a new identity: Norton I, Emperor of the United States. Until his death in 1880, Norton dressed in "imperial" regalia, issued proclamations, and handed out scrip—which was honored by San Francisco merchants. Ironically, he was more successful than ever.

Disorderly from the start, California's political history resists easy summarizing. At different times, the state has been governed by anarchy, populism, vigilantism, libertarianism, progressivism, and conservatism. It is the birthplace of both the Black Panther Party and the John Birch Society; its governors have included brilliant tacticians like Earl Warren (later chief justice of the Supreme Court) and genial crowd-pleasers like Ronald Reagan (later to be President). Even its capital city showed signs of restlessness, moving from Monterey to San Jose to Benicia to (finally) Sacramento.✸

Every Man for Himself

Lawlessness fueled by greed was the order of the day throughout early California. The mining camps were run by lynch law; San Francisco was destroyed by fire six times before 1851 because no one bothered to fund and form a municipal fire department. Street crime in 1870s San Francisco reached such extreme proportions that a new word, "hoodlum," was coined to describe its perpetrators. The Southern Pacific Railroad—"the Octopus" of Frank Norris's muck-raking novel—had an iron grip on every institution in the state. Reform came slowly, finally gaining the upper hand in 1910 when progressive Republican Hiram Johnson won the statehouse and pushed through the legislature the most sweeping reform package California had ever seen.

The Southern Pacific Railroad as octopus, in the satirical magazine *The Wasp. Bancroft Library. Opposite:* San Francisco's Vigilance Committee was activated in 1856 after the shooting of crusading editor James King by racketeer James Casey. *Wells Fargo Bank History Room*

"READY TO AVENGE AN INSULT, ACCUSTOMED TO CARRY pistols and knives, quick to use them in a quarrel."

John S. Hittell, describing the typical Californian in 1863

Labor Struggles

Organized labor in California first came not to the industrial assembly line but to the waterfront and the farm. And it came not by way of traditional labor movements but from the Communist Party. In 1933 Communist organizers formed the Cannery and Agricultural Workers' Union, which launched two dozen strikes in the San Joaquin Valley. On the waterfront, Australian-born Harry Bridges formed the International Longshoremen's Union in San Francisco, and when employers refused to recognize it, Bridges called a strike that tied up every port from San Diego to Seattle.

The resulting impasse led to the general strike of July 19, 1934, with 150,000 workers walking off their jobs in San Francisco. It took three months and federal mediation to force waterfront reforms.

Above: **Waterfront unionist Harry Bridges with his daughter in 1939, awaiting news on Bridges's deportation hearing.** *AP Photo/Underwood Photo Archives, SF. Right:* **Handbill for the IWW, the Wobblies, c. 1910.** *Far right:* **United Farm Workers benefit poster, Paul Davis Studio, c. 1968.** *Courtesy of the artist*

On the Ramparts

The famous uncredited photograph of Black Panther leader Huey Newton in his peacock chair, flanked by symbols of African pride, c. 1967. *The Doctor Huey P. Newton Foundation*

The 1960s, an explosive decade across the country, had its cultural epicenter in California. In Berkeley, the Free Speech Movement and later antiwar demonstrations galvanized the university community. In the largely black south-central Los Angeles enclave of Watts, tensions overflowed into street riots during the summer of 1965. The Black Panther Party, born in Oakland, gave dramatic voice to the pent-up anger of African-Americans. And in 1970, Native Americans took over the abandoned prison island of Alcatraz, occupying it for more than a year from 1969 to 1971 in an attempt to establish an Indian cultural center.

Left: Vice President and Mrs. Richard Nixon greet well-wishers in Oakland, 1960. *California Historical Society. Above:* The Great Communicator, President Ronald Reagan, in a campaign button for his 1984 reelection. *The Reagan Library*

In the first half of the 20th century, California asserted its growing wealth and stature by embarking on ambitious public works programs. A great system of dams, aqueducts, and pipelines brought water from the northern California mountains and from the Colorado River to the farming valleys and coastal cities. San Francisco spanned its bay with two famous bridges. Twice—in 1915 and 1939—California showed off its spirit of innovation in world fairs, which influenced architecture and design around the nation.

After the 1906 earthquake and fire leveled much of San Francisco, the city's rebuilding included Beaux Arts civic structures and an attempt (ultimately unsuccessful) to embody the "City Beautiful" movement. Public art received another boost in the WPA era: murals by noted painters were commissioned for civic buildings, and San Francisco's northern waterfront was trans-

Above: Hetch Hetchy Dam on the Tuolumne River, 1988. _Photo Barrie Rokeach. Below:_ The San Francisco Museum of Modern Art, designed by Swiss architect Mario Botta in 1987. _Photo Robert Holmes_

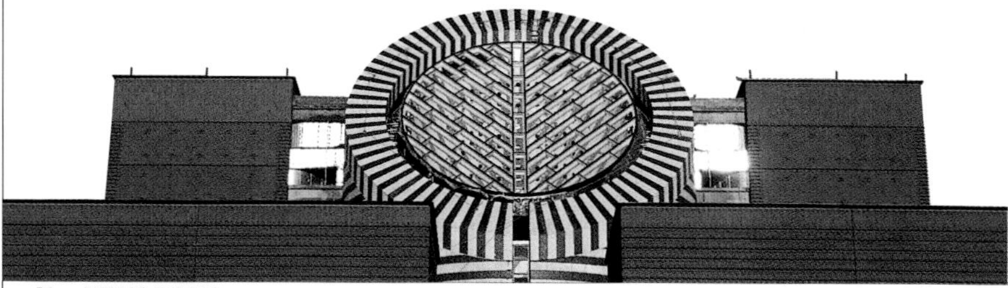

formed by a Streamline Moderne recreation complex. Since the 1960s, much of California's public building has been devoted to the arts: the L.A. Music Center; major art museums in Los Angeles, Oakland, and San Francisco; and regional performing arts centers in former suburbs have triumphantly overcome the state's lingering provincialism. However, to most of the world, California's most notable contribution to public works is also the bane of its existence: the justly praised, justly maligned freeways.✸

Freeway Interchange by Wayne Thiebaud, 1982. The artist's view is slightly exaggerated—but only slightly. *Campbell-Thiebaud Gallery*

"There it is. Take it."

William Mulholland, the engineer who diverted the Owens River to Los Angeles in 1913

Replacing stagecoaches with steam engines required a heroic effort and the sacrifice of many workers' lives. *Right: Snow Sheds on the Central Pacific Railroad in the Sierra Nevada Mountains* by Joseph Becker, c. 1870. *Gilcrease Museum. Below:* Stagecoach, c. 1850s. *Autry Museum of Western Heritage*

Linking the Continent

Cut off from the rest of the continent by the Sierra Nevada, California in the mid-19th century depended on agonizingly slow stagecoach and ship traffic for news, goods, and immigrants. Mail took seven or eight months to arrive from the East Coast. The hopes of progressive Californians lay in the building of a transcontinental railroad, but their dream was thwarted for years by topographical challenges and intrastate sectional politics. Paradoxically, the outbreak of the Civil War broke

the impasse. In 1862, Congress authorized construction of the railroad as a military necessity and a way to keep California on the Union side. Two lines—the Union Pacific from Omaha, using Irish workers, and the Central Pacific from California, employing Chinese—worked at an inhuman pace, against staggering odds. When they met at Promontory Point, Utah, in 1869, the continent was linked at last.

Cover of a 1949 pamphlet advertising the Western Pacific's famed California Zephyr. On board this train, it proclaimed, "every mile is a scenic thrill." ***California State Railroad Museum***

Great Expositions

Below: **Palace of Fine Arts, built in 1915 for San Francisco's Pan-Pacific Exposition. Hand-tinted photograph by Jules Guérin.** *Bottom:* **Buildings**

Completion of the Panama Canal in 1915 awakened Californians' dreams of world trade. To celebrate, the state held two spectacular expositions that year. San Diego, the first U.S. port of call for ships passing through the canal, sponsored the Panama-California Exposition; San Francisco held the "official" fair, the Panama-Pacific Exposition. The styles of each were outwardly as different as night and day—Bertram Goodhue's Spanish Baroque creations in sun-drenched Balboa Park seemed remote from Bernard Maybeck's ephemeral Beaux Arts structures on foggy San Francisco Bay. What united the events was their embrace of the new Arts and Crafts movement: a belief in harmony, simplicity, and natural materials. In 1939, to mark the opening of the Golden Gate and Oakland Bay bridges, San Francisco hosted another lavish party, the Golden Gate International Exposition. Its venue, Treasure Island,

in San Diego's Balboa Park were constructed for a rival exposition. *Photo Robert Holmes* *Opposite: Tower of the Sun* **by Chesley Bonestell, 1939. This painting by the noted science-fiction artist shows the tower as a polychrome beacon at night.** *Oakland Museum*

was created from the debris produced in building the Oakland span; its decor was fanciful, futuristic, and Asian-inspired.

Three times this century, California hosted the Olympic Games. Both Los Angeles Games occasioned major building projects, and the Winter Games of 1960 transformed Squaw Valley from a somnolent village to a world-class ski resort.

"I SAW THE VIBRANT TINTS of the native wild flowers, the soft browns of the surrounding hills, the gold of the orangeries, the blue of the sea; and I determined that, just as a musician builds his symphony around a motif or chord, so must I strike a chord of color and build my symphony on this."

Jules Guérin, "Chief of Color" for the Panama-Pacific Exposition

Golden Gate by Charles Sheeler, 1955. This skewed perspective conveys the majesty and drama of the Golden Gate Bridge, which spans one of the most spectacular waterways in the West. *Metropolitan Museum of Art. Below:* The San Francisco–Oakland Bay Bridge under construction, 1936. *California Historical Society. Photo Rovere Scott*

Lofty Spans, Working Waterfronts

The Golden Gate and Oakland Bay bridges, completed within two years of each other at the end of the Great Depression, were engineering marvels of their time. The Golden Gate Bridge, constructed amid churning currents in one of the most beautiful settings in the world, is San Francisco's trademark symbol. The double-deck San Francisco-Oakland Bay Bridge includes the world's only twin suspension span; yet its massiveness proved deceptive during the 1989 Loma Prieta earthquake. Lesser (but no less picturesque) bridges span the Sierra's mountain canyons and the Big Sur headlands.

Both before and after the railroad link,

California relied heavily on seagoing transport for immigration and trade. Swift Clipper ships of the mid-1800s brought goods around Cape Horn in just three months; steamers continued up the Sacramento River to the mining camps. Good natural harbors are scant on California's coast, so the best ones, San Francisco and San Diego, quickly became important centers of shipping and shipbuilding. Waterfront architecture tended to be utilitarian until Arthur Page Brown designed San Francisco's Ferry Building complex in 1895: a Roman Revival pavilion crowned by a clock tower modeled on the Cathedral of Seville. Today shipping remains vital in the southland and Oakland, while San Francisco's piers are mostly candidates for "adaptive reuse."

Victory Shipyards I by Erle Loran, 1945. World War II brought a huge influx of workers to California's shipyards and aircraft factories; many remained and contributed to the state's postwar population boom. *Anne Schechter and Reid Buckley*

California Classic and Modern

Early public architecture in California was shaped by haste, convenience, the abundance of wood for building, and the Victorian taste for embellishment. Around the turn of the century, the state's growing wealth drew architects from the East who set about creating more formally academic civic buildings in an eclectic range of styles including Renaissance, Romanesque, and Neoclassic. San Francisco's destructive 1906 quake gave Beaux-Arts-trained designers like Willis Polk a clean slate to create an outstanding Civic Center, and all of California's major cities boast fine Deco-era skyscrapers and distinguished university campuses.

Above: In the Los Angeles Main Library, artist Dean Cornwell and an assistant work on murals, completed in 1933, depicting California's past. Designed by Bertram Goodhue, the library was severely damaged by arson in 1986. The rebuilding maintained the distinctive pyramid roofline and restored the Arts and Crafts interiors. *Los Angeles Public Library*

Right: The dramatic central court of Los Angeles's Bradbury Building, built by George H. Wyman in 1893. Inspiration for the skylit court came from Edward Bellamy's *Looking Backward,* which described a utopian office building of the year 2000 as being "a vast hall full of light." *Julius Shulman*

The last quarter of the 20th century has seen the completion of many striking new projects, including the Museum of Contemporary Art in Los Angeles and San Francisco's MOMA and Center for the Arts. And there have been inventive solutions to the problem of bringing public libraries into the age of electronic information. Some of the most startling new work has come from the studio of Frank Gehry, a Los Angeles–based architect whose work spans private and public realms.

Architect Frank Gehry's work on the Aerospace Hall at the California Museum of Science and Industry in Los Angeles is a prime example of his gift for drama. It juxtaposes a plain stucco box with an enormous metal polygon; hovering over a 40-foot-high "hangar" door is a Lockheed F104 Starfighter jet, which serves as both exhibit and amusement. *Photo Michael Moran*

"IT WAS THE CLOSEST THING I'LL EVER GET TO DESIGNING A Gothic cathedral."

Architect Frank Gehry on his design for the California Aerospace Museum in Los Angeles's Exposition Park

One panel of the Works Progress Administration (WPA) murals in San Francisco's Coit Tower. During the Great Depression, the WPA put artists to work on public projects. *Photo Robert Holmes*

Painting the Towns

The historical connection between California and Mexico was reinforced in the early 1930s when Diego Rivera, José Orozco, and several other prominent Mexican muralists paid working visits to the state. Not only did they create important public art—Rivera contributed murals to the San Francisco Stock Exchange and the Golden Gate International Exposition—but they also influenced many local artists. Among the most notable examples of this influence are the Coit Tower murals, created by Californians Victor Arautoff, Clifford Wight, and others under the auspices of the Public Works of Art Project, and the murals at Rincon Annex, San Francisco's main post office (now a shopping/restaurant complex). More recent artists, especially from the Hispanic community, have carried on California's tradition of mural art, both indoors and out.

On the Wall

Notable mural art

in San Francisco

Diego Rivera, *Pan-American Unity*, City College

WPA murals, Coit Tower

Positively Fourth Street, Fort Mason

Carnaval, 24th Street (also Balmy Alley and other Mission District sites)

in southern California

Victor Clothing Co., downtown L.A.

Hollywood Jazz 1945–1972, Hollywood and Vine

Harbor Freeway Overture, downtown L.A.

Great Wall of Los Angeles, Van Nuys

Chicano Park, San Diego

Right: Nat King Cole, Billie Holiday, and Miles Davis star on the *Hollywood Jazz* mural, created in the 1980s by Richard Wyatt on the Capitol Records Building. *Photo Philip Corwin/Corbis. Below: Maestrapiece,* mural on the San Francisco Women's Building by Juana Alicia, Miranda Bergman, Edythe Boone, Susan Kelk Cervantes, Meera Desai, Yvonne Littleton, and Irene Perez, 1994. *Photo Cesar Rubio*

California's network of city, regional, state, and national parks spans a stunning range of native landscapes and wildlife as well as imported flora, recreational attractions, and decorative structures. Consider the private-turned-public Huntington Botanical Gardens, built early in the 20th century by the nephew of railroad baron Collis P. Huntington, which include a Japanese garden, an herb garden, and a Shakespeare garden (with plants mentioned in the Bard's plays)—all popular themes of the era. Another Shakespeare Garden is nestled in San Francisco's magnificent

Above: The Ahwanee Hotel, Yosemite National Park. *Photo Julius Shulman. Right:* Huntington Gardens, San Marino. *Photo Ken Druse. Opposite above:* Golden Gate Park's Conservatory was prefabricated and shipped around Cape Horn. *Photo Richard Sexton. Opposite below:* Japanese Tea Garden, Golden Gate Park. *Photo Andrew McKinney*

Golden Gate Park, whose 1,000-plus acres were reclaimed from sand dunes; the park also contains the Conservatory (one of the finest surviving Victorian glass follies) and a Japanese Tea Garden constructed for the 1894 California Midwinter International Exposition. Griffith Park, near downtown Los Angeles, sprawls across 4,107 acres in the Santa Monica Mountains. Its observatory, familiar to fans of the 1955 film *Rebel Without a Cause*, provides a fine vantage for viewing both city and celestial lights. Farther south, Balboa Park is a 1,158-acre cultural mecca in the heart of San Diego. Many of the original exhibit halls, designed in ornate Spanish Colonial and Churrigueresque styles, are still in use. The park also encompasses the famous San Diego Zoo, one of the world's largest. ✸

Two seemingly contradictory themes converge, and sometimes conflict, in California life. The first is the impulse to integrate indoors and outdoors, to live harmoniously with nature. It's almost impossible to speak of the California home without reference to California gardens, and the use of natural materials in structures and objects that echo natural forms has been a dominant theme through several eras. The second is the state's characteristic urge toward fantasy and reinvention, which finds expression in everything from Mother Goose architecture to candy-flake hot rods to surrealistic swimming pools.✹

In the Victorian Style

During the last three decades of the 19th century, the emerging middle class and nouveau riche set off a residential building boom throughout California, particularly in the north. California's builders were blessed by an abundance of wood, especially redwood, and they rose to the occasion with a phantasmagoria of millwork. Stick Victorian, Eastlake, Queen Anne, and Romanesque styles merged flamboyantly, often in the same building. Although these building styles were popular elsewhere in the country during the period, California (and particularly San Francisco) stands alone in its fanciful use of colorful exteriors.

"THE IMITATION OF CHATEAUX AND COPIES of fragments of palaces, carried out in thin, wooden, box-like structures...."

Noted turn-of-the-century architect Arthur Page Brown, dismissing the Victorian style so revered today

Opposite: Ladies in the Garden by Arthur F. Matthews, 1923. *The Buck Collection. Above:* Italianate row house. *Right:* Parlor in a San Francisco Victorian-era house. San Francisco's Victorian houses, with their gracefully attenuated proportions and elaborate millwork, are almost as much of a city symbol as the Golden Gate Bridge. *Photos Richard Sexton*

THE AGELESS GRACE OF ARTS AND CRAFTS

"Simplicity, significance, utility, harmony–these are the watchwords!"

Berkeley architect Charles Keeler, 1909

Right: **Three-light lotus lamp of abalone and hammered brass by Elizabeth Eaton Burton, c. 1935.** *Collection of Isak Lindenauer. Below:* **Desk of carved and painted wood by Arthur and Lucia Mathews, 1910–12.** *Oakland Museum*

From the 1890s to the 1930s, California experienced a flowering of original architecture and craft. The Craftsman style, with its emphasis on natural materials and honest feeling, was first articulated by two Englishmen, John Ruskin and William Morris. Many of their American followers, including Willis Polk, Gustav Stickley, and Bernard Maybeck, migrated to California, where there was opportunity, as Stickley put it, to create "a truer democracy than anything in the Middle or Eastern part of America." Like the Victorians, the Craftsmen used native redwood—but left it natural and unpainted, often with beams and other architectural elements exposed. In pottery, garden design, and metalwork, they brought a spiritual idealism to their work that opposed modern industrialization. Yet it was sophisticated machinery that enabled these designers to produce such a large body of work.✸

The California Bungalow

Although its name comes from a Hindi word, the California "bungalow" is a truly indigenous creation. It was developed in Southern California, where its overhanging eaves, flat roof, broad porch, and low windows suited the desert climate. But as it was cheap to build, it took hold elsewhere in the state, notably the Bay Area, where wood shingles replaced stucco. Between 1904 and 1910, the Pasadena architectural firm of Greene & Greene designed the "ultimate bungalows": the Gamble house (for a scion of the Procter & Gamble family), the Pratt house, the Blacker house, and— in Berkeley—the Thorsen house.

Architects Charles Sumner Greene and Henry Mather Greene, originally from Ohio, created their "ultimate bungalows" in California. *Above:* Entry hall of the David B. Gamble House, Pasadena, completed in 1908. Handsomely suited to its environment, it is the best-preserved of the Greene & Greene bungalows. *Photo Steve Smith/West Light*

Clearing Storm, Santa Barbara by Richard Schloss, 1995. Santa Barbara's Spanish Revival architecture gives the city its look of a fantasy Mediterranean village by the sea. *Courtesy of the artist. Below:* the Roman pool at Hearst Castle, designed by Julia Morgan. *Photo Fred Lyon*

Shades of the Mediterranean

Sparked by Helen Hunt Jackson's 1884 romance of the missions, *Ramona,* and by Charles Fletcher Lummis's campaign to restore the San Fernando Mission, the Mission Revival movement transformed southern California's architectural landscape and made headway in the north as well. It paved the way for the more elaborate Spanish Colonial Revival of the late teens and '20s. Californian Julia Morgan, the first female architecture graduate of the Ecole des Beaux-Arts in Paris, took Spanish Colonial Revival style to its dizzying summit in her design for "Hearst Castle." This splendid mansion, perched on a hillside above San Simeon on the central coast, was created to house the treasures of publisher William Randolph Hearst. Morgan modeled its towers after a church in Ronda, Spain, and incorporated Egyptian, Greek, and Roman antiquities into her design.

Coastal Contemporary

While American-born designers were resurrecting the Spanish past, a group of European exiles was pioneering a new, modern style for California. The work of Rudolf Schindler and Richard Neutra in the south and Eric Mendelsohn in San Francisco adapted the International Style to local climate and materials: flat roofs (it didn't snow), stucco walls (a nod to the adobe missions), and lots of glass (for the wonderful views). Streamlined designs also characterize furniture and housewares of the period. Some was kitsch, some soared beyond, as in the groundbreaking furniture of Charles and Ray Eames, the husband-wife team who worked in California from 1941 on. The latest wave of contemporary architecture, exemplified by Frank Gehry and Brian Murphy, is deliberately startling, intended to clash with the landscape rather than blend in. This trend toward hard-edged reality seems to represent a turning away from the romantic lifestyle designs of California's past.

Above: **Chaise designed by Charles O. Eames and Ray Eames for their friend, director Billy Wilder, 1968.** *Herman Miller, Inc. Photo Nick Merrick ©Hedrich Blessing*
Right: **Tiburon B, a contemporary house designed by Philippe Banta on San Francisco Bay with lap pool for serious swimming.** *Photo Andrew McKinney*

The Organic Impulse

During the 1960s and 1970s, the design pendulum swung briefly back to the "handmade" aesthetic, at least among a small group of Californians who were exploring a more "natural," anticorporate lifestyle. On the high-culture end of the spectrum were a renaissance in ceramics, other crafts, and craftsman-style architecture (Narsai's, an haute California restaurant, had inner walls made from recycled redwood wine barrels). On the low-culture end were coffee tables crafted from burlwood and a variety of handmade houses.

Above: A handmade house in the "woodbutchered" style, designed in 1970 by Valentino Agnoli at Stinson Beach. *Photo James Martin. Right: Jabo* by Peter Voulkos, 1994. Voulkos is known for his monumental ceramic pieces; this wood-fired stoneware stack stands 42 inches tall. *Kenji Taki Gallery. Photo Hiromu Narita*

Couch and Chair with Landscape and Cows by Richard Shaw, 1966–67. *American Craft Museum*

Below: The famous bus "Furthur" [*sic*], on which Ken Kesey and the Merry Pranksters made their epic 1960s road trips, at the 1965 Acid Test in San Francisco. *Photo Gene Anthony*

Funk and Flash

From fashion to front yards to art galleries, California tolerates eccentricity with considerable good humor. The Zoot Suit fad of the 1940s reached its apotheosis in L.A.'s Mexican-American *barrio;* hippie spangles and fringes were most splendiferous in San Francisco's Haight-Ashbury. Removed from the rest of the continent, fine artists also were liberated to explore whimsical, playful directions.

"THERE WERE VERY MANY PECULIAR THINGS stuck randomly around [Kesey's] property: human skulls, incomprehensible signs.... Many objects had been painted in the slightly poisonous pink and green shades of fluorescent Day-Glo...."

Charles Perry, The Haight-Ashbury, *1984*

Filoli, in the San Francisco Peninsula town of Woodside, is among California's and the nation's most splendid gardens. Famed as the setting of TV's *Dynasty,* it was created beginning in 1915 by William Bourn II in the style of Irish Georgian gardens and is now owned by the National Trust. Its 16 acres include this Mediterranean garden as well as sunken and walled gardens in a landscape of wooded hills. *Photo Felix Rigau. Opposite above:* Ruth Bancroft's southern California cactus and succulent garden. *Photo Gentl & Hyers Opposite below:* The poolside patio of a Heidi Richardson–designed garden against the backdrop of Napa Valley. *Photo Andrew McKinney*

California's indigenous peoples were not cultivators, but nearly everyone who followed them was. Introduced species such as palm trees, camellias, and roses grew prolifically in California's benign climate, and early gardens were simply collections of exotic wonders. Later, gardeners and landscape architects began to incorporate views of the surrounding landscape, and to create of the garden a true outdoor living space. Integral to this concept was the patio, which allowed an easy transition between indoors and outdoors.

In the late 19th and early 20th century, the gardens of California's rich and powerful were modeled after European examples, in particular English country estates.

Filoli, the Woodside estate of millionaire arts patron William Bourn, represents the urge to tame Nature into an orderly, "cultured" ideal; its 16 acres of gardens include formal topiaries and hedges, tens of thousands of bulbs and annuals, and more than 220 barrel-shaped Irish yews. In southern California, influences tended to come from Spain; George Washington Smith created many memorable Santa Barbara gardens in the 1920s, including "Casa del Herrero," with its Alhambra-influenced courtyard and tile ornamentation. ✹

"ON MY OWN LITTLE PLACE THERE ARE, TODAY, AT LEAST FORTY MILLION WILD BLOSSOMS, by my calculation. Short of the wandering and unconventional foot-paths...you cannot step anywhere without trampling flowers— maybe ten to a step, as a minimum. One bred to climes where God counts flowers as Easterners do their copper cents, may not prefer to walk on them; but out here God and we can afford the carpet."

Charles Fletcher Lummis, 1905

Without leaving Orange County, a visitor can be dazzled by fairy-tale fantasy—or state-of-the-art thrills. *Below:* Fireworks display over Sleeping Beauty's Castle, Disneyland. *Photo Dewitt Jones* *Right:* The Boomerang roller coaster at Knott's Berry Farm, Buena Park. *Photo Robert Holmes*

Play is serious business in California. Where else can you surf on the coast, play tennis in the desert, and ski in the mountains within one 24-hour day? More significantly, where else would such activities be considered reasonable and appropriate for grown-ups? In coming to California, people often abandoned old ideas about work and responsibility; for better or worse, this outlook created a recreational paradise.✸

Festivals and Fantasylands

Before 1955, amusement parks were often unsavory places where admission was free but every booth offered a chance to lose money. Walt Disney reversed the formula. Disneyland, his 160-acre dream park in Anaheim, was spotless and upbeat: "the happiest place on earth." Customers, called "guests," paid

California's Chinese celebrations are well established; the Brazilian connection is more latter-day. *Left: Chinese New Year Parade* by Martin Wong, 1992. *Photo P.P.O.W., New York* *Below:* A samba school struts its stuff at Carnival in San Francisco's Mission District. *Photo Robert Holmes*

steep entrance prices but many of the attractions were free. Other parks attempted to duplicate the Disney magic, with varying success. An Orange County neighbor, Knott's Berry Farm, added sophisticated rides. Universal Studios opened its doors to visitors by the tramload. And San Diego's Sea World set the pattern for water shows featuring thrilling marine mammal acts.

Everyone loves a parade, none more than Golden Staters. To the great American tradition of holiday parades, California has contributed unique spectacles such as Pasadena's Rose Parade and San Francisco's Chinese New Year and Gay Pride parades. And its sun shines on outdoor festivals great and small: street fairs, music and art shows, ethnic celebrations, Renaissance reenactments, and food-based events like Gilroy's fragrant Garlic Festival.

The population boom and freewheeling freeway construction transformed the California autoscape in less than seven decades. *Right:* Cover from *The California Motorist,* August 1918. *American Automobile Association. Below: Downtown* by Frank Romero, 1990. Romero first gained attention in the 1970s as a member of "Los Four," a Los Angeles-based group of socially and politically committed Chicanos. *Courtesy of the artist*

John Muir explored California on foot, but even in his time he was unusual. From the days of *rancheros* on horseback, Californians have preferred faster means of locomotion. Car camping was popular as early as the 1920s, and the first "motor courts" appeared around the same time. It was a Californian who coined the word "motel,"

and though drive-in theaters were invented elsewhere, California led the way with drive-through banks, restaurants, even funeral parlors. Hot-rodding was born here, too, on the southland's dry lakebeds and Mojave Desert hard-

Hot-rodding spawned a style and vocabulary of its own. A "Deuce Coupe" got its name from the "2" in "1932," for the Ford V-8 model of that year. "Candy apple" referred to a paint application created in the early 1950s that simulated the shimmering coating on a candied apple. *Left: The California Kid,* 1934 Ford Coupe built by Pete Chapouris. *Collection Jerry Slover. Below:* Hell on wheels—Marlon Brando astride his motorcycle in *The Wild One,* 1955. *Ron Borst/ Hollywood Movie Posters*

pan in 1920s. It took off after World War II, when a used Model T or Model A could be had for practically nothing and customized into a flashy race car. Oakland native Tommy "The Greek" Hrones, Sacramentan Ed Ohanesian, L.A.'s Gil Ayala, and Dick "Magoo" Megugorac—the hot-rod culture cuts across ethnic, class, and generational lines, uniting designers, builders, and car owners in a mutual passion for speed and flash.✸

"THE MAIN THING YOU NOTICE IS THE COLOR—TANGERINE flake. This paint—one of Barris' Kandy Kolor concoctions—makes the car look like it has been encrusted with chips of some kind of semi-precious ossified tangerine, all coated with a half-inch of clear lacquer."

Tom Wolfe, The Kandy-Kolored Tangerine Flake Streamlined Baby, *1965*

Famous for his Gold Rush stories, Bret Harte was an important figure on California's early literary scene. In 1868, Harte and Oakland

librarian Ina Coolbrith founded *The Overland Monthly*, which in its brief flowering published many California writers and cast a beckoning spell across the country. *Bancroft Library*
Right: Jack London's bookplate with his signature wolf, drawn by E. J. Cross

"I COULD SEE PEOPLE LIVING—AMID MAGNIFICENT SCENERY—essentially as they did in the Idyls or the Sagas, or in Homer's Ithaca. Here was life purged of its ephemeral accretions."

Robinson Jeffers, from his introduction to Selected Poetry, 1927

Far from the Eastern establishment, free from constraints, California was a haven for creative souls pursuing dreams of self-expression. The state's literary roster is rich in nonconformists, from Joaquin Miller and Ambrose Bierce to Jack London and George Sterling, from Robinson Jeffers to Henry Miller, Gary Snyder, and Ursula LeGuin. The familiar themes—the search for a terrestrial Eden, attachment to the land, desire for transformation—also found expression in theater and dance. Along with bohemians and beatniks, California has fostered a rich chorus of ethnic voices—Hispanic, Asian, Armenian—whose writings offer a clear counterpoint to the California Dream. Throughout this century, the state also attracted expatriate writers whose commentaries on the Golden State have been both astute and acerbic: it is hard to imagine literary California without Jessica Mitford, Aldous Huxley, Christopher Isherwood, and Evelyn Waugh.✸

Shown here preparing for a 1907 theatrical production is poet George Sterling, the unofficial guru of turn-of-the-century Carmel. Other denizens of the artistic seaside community included Mary Austin, who set up a writing studio in a treehouse, and Upton Sinclair. *Below:* Poet Robinson Jeffers, a later bard of the central coast, bronze by Jo Davidson, c. 1930s. ***Both, Bancroft Library***

Bohemians and Beats

Writers and free thinkers found California a haven of tolerance. In 1872 a group of San Francisco journalists founded the Bohemian Club, which acquired a stylish notoriety. The poet Joaquin Miller, artists Virgil Williams and Julian Rix, and Berkeley scientist Joseph Le Conte all were members; when Oscar Wilde visited, he was entertained by the Bohemians. South of San Francisco, an arts colony took shape on the windswept Monterey Peninsula.

Less convivial but more influential was Jack London, born in San Francisco in 1876. Despite his robust early adventures in Alaska and the South Seas, London was often ill and haunted by insecurity. Alienated from his real world,

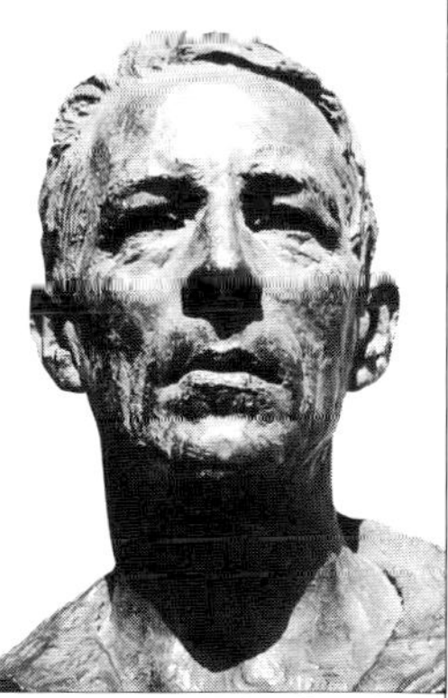

he immersed himself in a mythical California past and died at his Sonoma ranch at age 40. The Beats of the 1950s were, in a sense, his spiritual descendants. In San Francisco's North Beach, poets like Lawrence Ferlinghetti, Gregory Corso, Philip Whalen, and Diane di Prima held public readings—often in Ferlinghetti's bookstore mecca, City Lights—intended to bring poetry out of the ivory tower and into the streets.

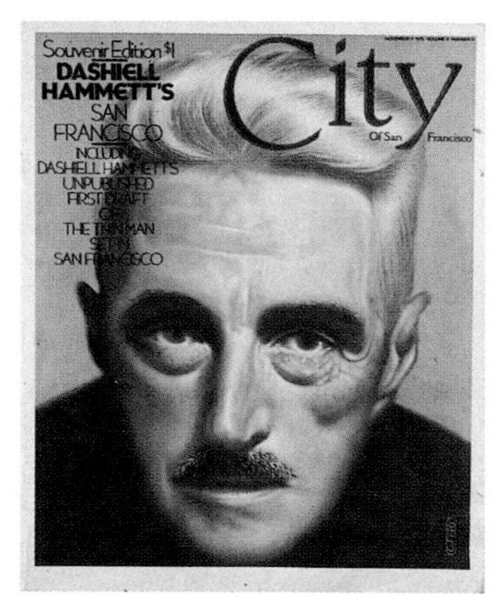

Urban Noir

The great practitioners of the hard-boiled detective story were all at least temporarily Californians, and this was the setting for their most famous work. Dashiell Hammett established the Continental Op and Sam Spade as archetypes of the dark, moody, action-packed crime novel. In classics like *The Postman Always Rings Twice* and *Mildred Pierce,* James M. Cain introduced Hollywood yearnings and southern California landscapes to the genre. Raymond Chandler's Philip Marlowe novels roam through Los Angeles of the 1930s to '50s, from downtown jail cells to swanky nightclubs. Jim Thompson wrote chilling pulp tales that plumbed the minds of the criminally insane. Ross Macdonald brought noir fiction into the postwar era of suburbs and tennis courts, and Walter Mosley mines it from L.A.'s black community.

"ON NIGHTS LIKE THAT, EVERY BOOZE PARTY ENDS IN A FIGHT. Meek little wives feel the edge of the carving knife and study their husbands' necks. Anything can happen."

Raymond Chandler on the effect of the Santa Ana wind, in "Red Wind," 1939

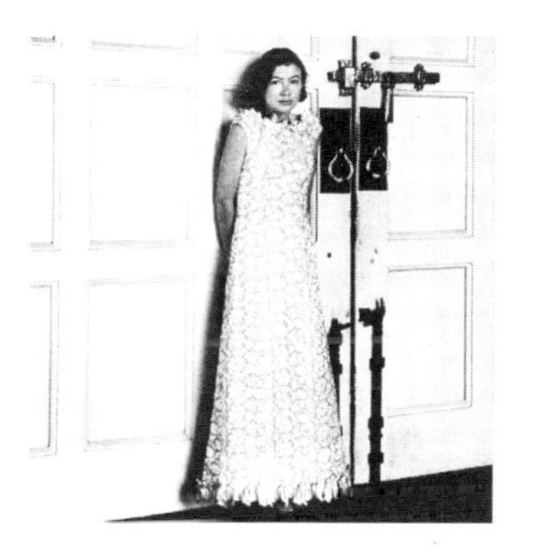

"SHE DROVE THE SAN DIEGO TO THE Harbor, the Harbor up to the Hollywood, the Hollywood to the Golden State, the Santa Monica, the Santa Ana, the Pasadena, the Ventura. She drove it as a riverman runs a river, every day more attuned to its currents, its deceptions, and just as a riverman feels the pull of the rapids in the lull between sleeping and waking, so Maria lay at night and saw the great signs soar overhead at seventy miles an hour, *Normandie 1/4 Vermont 3/4 Harbor Fwy 1*."

Joan Didion, Play It As It Lays, *1970*

Opposite above: Illustration of Dashiell Hammett by Guy Fery, in the November 1975 *City* magazine, published by Francis Ford Coppola. *Courtesy David Fechheimer* *Opposite below: Self Portrait* by Henry Miller, 1962. *Collection of Gary Koeppel. Top:* Joan Didion, 1964. *Bancroft Library. Photo Dominick Dunne. Above: The one who comes to question himself* by Kenneth Patchen, c. 1966. *University of California, Santa Cruz, Special Collections*

As early as the Gold Rush, nearly every self-respecting California town could boast a theater or opera house (towns with Chinese populations often had Chinese opera as well). The theatrical arts, robust and often iconoclastic, continued to flourish after statehood. No performing artist better exemplified the freewheeling spirit of the early 20th century than Isadora Duncan, the child of a San Francisco banker. Taking inspiration from Nature, classical Greece, and the California epic, Duncan virtually founded modern dance. California has also wielded much influence in contemporary drama. Luis Valdez's Teatro Campesino merges traditional *corridas* with topical *barrio* and farmworker issues; the San Francisco Mime Troupe marries commedia dell'arte forms and radical politics; the Mark Taper Theater in Los Angeles introduces serious new playwrights to sophisticated audiences. And San Francisco's long-running *Beach Blanket Babylon* amuses locals and visitors alike with its over-the-top parodies.✸

"I BRING YOU THE DANCE. I BRING YOU THE idea that is going to revolutionise [*sic*] our entire epoch. Where have I discovered it? By the Pacific Ocean, by the waving pine-forests of Sierra Nevada."

Isadora Duncan in her autobiography, 1927

Opposite above: Program cover for the California Theatre, March 1900. *Opposite below:* Isadora Duncan, c. 1905. *Both, San Francisco Performing Arts Library & Museum. Left:* The San Francisco Mime Troupe performs *13 Dias/13 Days—How the New Zapatistas Shook the World,* 1994. *SF Mime Troupe. Photo Mark Estes. Below left:* Val Diamond wears the city of San Francisco in Steve Silver's *Beach Blanket Babylon.* *© Steve Silver Productions, Inc. Below:* John Goodman as Falstaff in the Old Globe Theatre's production of *Henry IV,* 1995. *Old Globe Theatre. Photo Ken Howard*

Early American and European visitors to California remarked on the fondness of Spanish-Mexican *rancheros* for music and dancing. Weddings, harvests, holidays—all were occasions to pick up a guitar and castanets and dance the fandango or contradanza. The Forty-Niners brought their own raucous ballads, but also a touch of high culture. Regular opera performances were given in San Francisco as early as 1851, and remote mining towns hosted concerts by traveling musicians. Popular music, too, has a rich

Above: The Banjo Player by Maynard Dixon, 1901. *Autry Museum of Western Heritage. Right:* Mariachi band in San Francisco's Cinco de Mayo Parade. *Photo Bonnie Kamin*

history in the state. Latin-based folk music has been continually renewed by migrants from Mexico and Central America. The Southern blacks who came to work in the shipyards during World War II brought blues, jazz, and a dance style that came to be known as West Coast Swing, which was slower and more sensual than the jitterbug. In the Central Valley, around Bakersfield, Dust Bowl refugees created a uniquely Californian flavor of country-western music; their urban counterparts like the Eagles turned the sound into 1970s country rock.✹

Left: **Chinese Opera performer in typically elaborate costume, c. late 19th century.** *San Francisco Performing Arts Library & Museum. Below:* **Album cover photo for** ***Jazz West Coast*** **by William Claxton, 1957.** *Courtesy of the artist*

"IT WAS THE WINTER OF 1949. . . . WE WOULD stay up late listening to the records of the young Sarah Vaughan, Dizzy Gillespie, and of course, Bird. I think that we wore out all of Charlie Parker's Dial recordings. We would drive around Hollywood in a Cadillac convertible late at night in the rain and scat sing Bird's solos. . . ."

Jazz photographer William Claxton, 1992

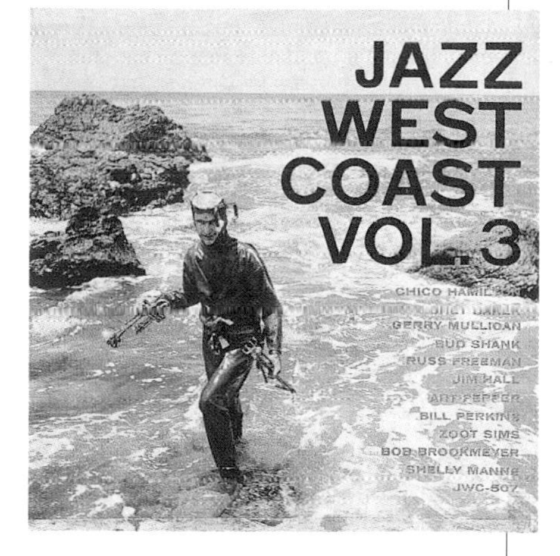

High and Low Tones

California, especially the Bay Area, was the epicenter of the musical explosion of the 1960s. The Jefferson Airplane, the Grateful Dead, Country Joe and the Fish, and Big Brother and the Holding Company (with singer Janis Joplin) regaled flower children with acid rock and electrified covers of classic blues. The mass concert made history here: the Beatles at Candlestick Park, the Rolling Stones at Altamont. A distinctive visual style, shaped by Art Nouveau and LSD hallucinations, accompanied the music: concert posters and album covers displayed pulsing colors and sinuous, nearly illegible letterforms.

"Highbrow music" continued to flourish, with San Francisco's opera company growing into world-class stature. In the 1930s and '40s, Los Angeles hosted an expatriate community of European exiles, including Igor Stravinsky, Paul Hindemith, and Arnold Schoenberg, who taught

Left: California bluesman Robert Cray in a 1992 performance. *Photo Jack Vartoogian. Above:* The Grateful Dead emerged from the San Francisco Peninsula in the early 1960s and went on to become a national phenomenon during the hippie era and beyond. Poster, *Grateful Dead at the Avalon Ballroom* by Stanley Mouse, 1966. *Family Dog Productions*

Vinyl California, a Partial Discography

California, Here I Come

I Love You, California

California Girls

California Dreamin'

Hotel California

(If You Go to) San Francisco (Be Sure to Wear Some Flowers in Your Hair)

I Left My Heart in San Francisco

(They Say) It Never Rains in California

(If I Could Just Get Off of) That L.A. Freeway

West Coast Blues

My California

Santa Catalina ("26 Miles Across the Sea")

at UCLA. Later, L.A. native John Cage made waves with his experimental compositions. The Bay Area's Henry Cowell, Ernst Bacon (a 1932 Pulitzer Prize winner), and Roy Harris made enduring reputations. Today, John Adams in Berkeley and Lou Harrison in Santa Cruz continue the tradition, blending eastern and western influences in their musical works. And San Francisco Symphony music director Michael Tilson Thomas collaborates with Grateful Dead bassist Phil Lesh in the sacred precincts of Davies Symphony Hall.

Above: **David Hockney's set for the San Francisco Opera's 1993 production of *Turandot. San Francisco Opera. Photo Marty Sohl. Left:* California composer Henry Cowell in an illustration by Tim Bower, 1997. *The New Yorker***

"The only way to avoid Hollywood is to live there."

Igor Stravinsky

Vintage postcard of Hollywood Boulevard in the 1920s. *Courtesy Jim Heimann. Below:* Marilyn Monroe, archetypal Hollywood star, in 1953. *Superstock. Opposite above:* Poster for *Hondo,* starring John Wayne, 1953. *Ron Borst/Hollywood Movie Posters*

Haute Hollywood

Just as Hollywood created dreams for export, so it created fantasies for domestic consumption. The fabulous mansions of stars like Joan Crawford, Dick Powell, and Fred Astaire—with swimming pools, tennis courts, waterfalls, and private golf courses—were the stuff of daydreams for countless moviegoers, who conflated "real life" with "the pictures." As the home of the movies, Hollywood created the most elaborate movie palaces in the world: fantastically themed edifices like Graumann's (now Mann's) Chinese Theater and the Egyptian Theater, where movie premieres became thrilling community events. Hotels, restaurants, even cemeteries shared in the glamour—and the whimsy. Today the studio system is defunct and "the movies" are "the entertainment industry," but around the world the fantasy still works its seductive magic: to be bigger than life, richer than Croesus, more powerful than presidents and kings...if only for 90 minutes in a darkened theater.

"AN ENTIRE GENERATION OF ASPIRING MIDDLE-class Americans took its cues in the matter of domestic living from what Mary Pickford and Douglas Fairbanks were up to at Pickfair, their Beverly Hills estate. [They] and their Hollywood peers took the message of Southern California to the rest of the nation. Not even orange crate labels had a comparable influence."

Kevin Starr, Inventing the Dream, *1985*

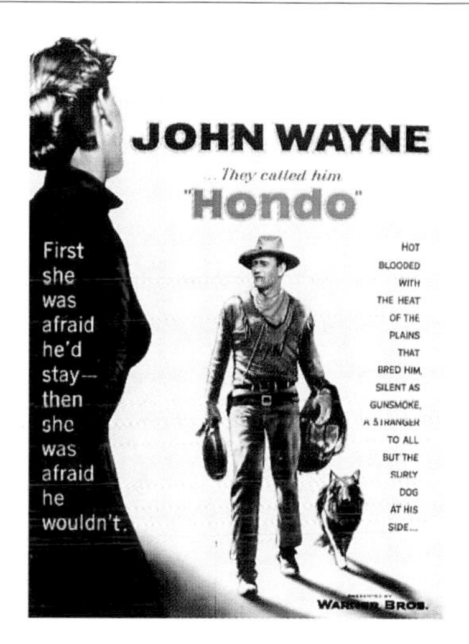

Below: **Robert A. M. Stern's 1994 design for the Disney Studio's Feature Animation Building in Burbank brings whimsy down to earth.** ***Walt Disney Imagineering. Photo Peter Aaron/Esto***

Trademark 3 by Ed Ruscha, 1962. *Collection of the artist. Opposite: Ocean Park No. 70* by Richard Diebenkorn, 1974. *Des Moines Art Center. Photo Michael Tropea.* During the same decades, using distinctly different styles, Ruscha and Diebenkorn reflected the clear light and familiar iconography of southern California. Diebenkorn began his *Ocean Park* series in 1967, naming the large oil paintings after the section of Santa Monica beach where he lived.

Modernism was already the "art of the state" by the 1930s when Group f.64, led by Ansel Adams, Imogen Cunningham, and Edward Weston, established new and influential perspectives in photography. Weston lived for a time with the painter Henrietta Shore, who in 1916 founded the Los Angeles Modern Art Society and established herself as a leading California modernist. Other early modernists include Danish-born Knud Merrild, whose work influenced a later generation of assemblage artists, and the Bay Area's Charles Howard, with his close affinity for Surrealism. In the post–World War II decades, Bay Area painters Richard Diebenkorn, Elmer Bischoff, and David Park developed distinctive styles of Abstract Expressionism, while Wayne Thiebaud and William Wiley used realism as a springboard.✸

Terrace, Hollywood Hills House with Banana Tree by David Hockney, 1982. The English-born Hockney has been closely identified with Los Angeles, and especially its emblematic swimming pools, since the 1960s. *Courtesy of the artist*

Bay Area Figurative painting, developed by Bischoff and Park before they turned to abstraction, found a distinctively quirky exponent in Joan Brown, whose emphasis on domestic subjects set her apart. In southern California, British expatriate David Hockney found lyric symbolism in backyard swimming pools, while Ed Ruscha elevated mundane urban streetscapes to mythic dimensions. Diebenkorn's most famous canvases, the "Ocean Park" series, also were made after the artist relocated to southern California.

"WHILE THE ART TREND IN THE east continues toward an assimilated union of modernism and conservatism, . . . across the continent in San Francisco the more radical phases of aesthetic experience maintain their hold. . . . San Francisco may well be called the capital of ultra-modern art in America."

Art Digest, *1941*

Left: California Artist by Robert Arneson, 1983. Arneson's three-dimensional self-portraits combine irony and exuberance in what might be called an only-in-California style. *The Estate of Robert Arneson* *Above: After the Alcatraz Swim #3* by Joan Brown, 1976. Brown, an avid open-water swimmer, often incorporated tiny swimmers in the vastness of San Francisco Bay into her 1960s work. Her ever-evolving vision was cut short by her accidental death in 1990. *Palm Springs Desert Museum*

California continues to experiment and pioneer in all forms of culture, from popular entertainment to graphic design, from conceptual art to multicultural theater and dance. Sculptors Mark di Suvero, Manuel Neri, Viola Frey, and Clayton Bailey have stretched the limits of their media, and environmental artist Christo has produced some of his most memorable works in California. Mixed media, with its rich layers of content, achieves unusual subtlety in the hands of Raymond Saunders, Betye and Alison Saar, Hung Liu, and others. Installations have

Opposite above: Glacier Vessel by John Lewis, 1997. Berkeley native Lewis pioneered the use of cast glass in sculptural and architectural contexts. *Courtesy of the artist. Opposite below: Denny's Arco* by Stephen Hopkins, 1987. Painting in a Photorealist style, Hopkins particularizes the California urbanscape. *Modernism, Inc. Left: Things were never $1.50* by Raymond Saunders, 1995. Working in Oakland and Venice, Saunders combines references to his African-American heritage with other sources. *Courtesy of the artist and Stephen Wirtz Gallery. Photo Charles Frizzell*

taken center stage in many galleries and museum shows, and performance art has made a canvas of the artist's self, merging a fine-arts orientation with voice, movement, and physical transformation and bringing this hybrid to venues beyond traditional art spaces. Meanwhile, young artists working in the new media of video, CD-ROM, and the Internet—in Silicon Valley and in home studios—are exploring a new frontier at the interface of art and technology.✸

Running Fence, Sonoma and Marin Counties, California by Christo, 1972–76. The Bulgarian-born artist used entire landscapes as his canvases. For just two weeks, his *Running Fence*, an 18-foot-high banner of white nylon, snaked across 24½ miles of northern California terrain, changing with light and weather and heightening a viewer's experience of the land's contours. *Photo Bruce Lauritzen*

SFMOMA by Robin Winfield, 1996. By altering her Cibachrome photographic images with acrylics, Winfield celebrates architectural form and manipulates mood. This image explores the interior of San Francisco's new modern art museum. The young artist, based in Carmel, also works in photo-collage, textiles, and wearable art. *Courtesy of the artist*

"CALIFORNIA BECAME, AS IT HAD TO, THE NEW WORLD'S NEW WORLD, its last repository of hope. In California, you come face to face with the Pacific and yourself. There is nowhere else to go.... All that California does is magnify what is brought to it; and often, under the strain of magnification, there occurs a sea change."

Shiva Naipaul, Journey to Nowhere: A New World Tragedy, *1980*

American Buddha* by Arthur Okamura, 1994. Recent work by this Asian-American painter depicts Buddhas within mystical landscapes.** ***Braunstein/Quay Gallery

Watts Towers

Between 1921 and 1954 an Italian immigrant, Simon Rodia, single-handedly created one of the most singular folk-art structures anywhere on earth: eight spidery, concrete-encased steel towers embedded with shells, tile, pottery shards, and glass. In south-central Los Angeles, they can be toured on weekends.

Star Gazing

Hollywood is not the only place in California to see stars. The 200-inch Hale telescope at the Palomar Observatory, northeast of Escondido, is capable of viewing a billion light years into the universe. Visitors can see an outstanding collection of space photos. In northern California, the place to go is the Lick Observatory, on 4,209-foot Mt. Hamilton, east of San Jose.

Appearing at the Paramount...

One of the state's most striking examples of Art Deco, this Timothy Pfluger-designed Oakland theatrical palace was built as a movie theater in 1931 and restored four decades later. It houses concerts, screenings, and the Oakland Ballet.

A Sticky Subject

A bit of the Pleistocene Ice Age survives on L.A.'s Wilshire Boulevard. Here in the La Brea Tar Pits, unsuspecting woolly mammoths, saber-tooth cats, and giant ground sloths, mistaking a giant tar pit for a watering hole,

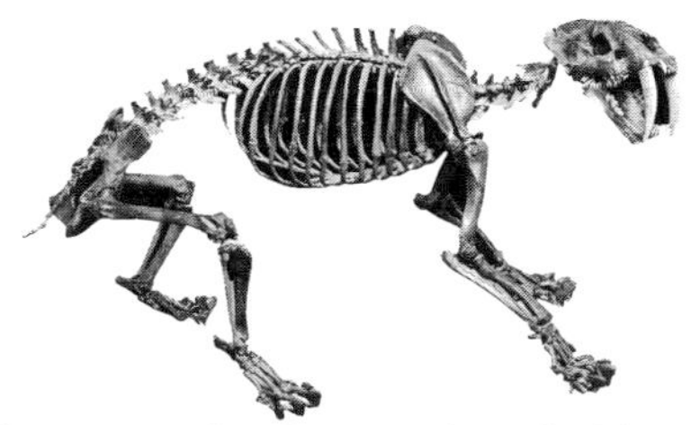

became mired in the goo and perished there. Today that tar pit, still bubbling, is one of the world's richest sources of ice-age fossils.

Winchester Mystery House

Sarah Winchester, widow of the rifle inventor, kept adding on to her unfinished San Jose mansion, believing that as long as she kept building she would stay alive. With 160 rooms, 2,000 doors, and countless secret passageways, even Mrs. Winchester needed a map.

Outsized Appetites

California, especially the southland, has never been shy or subtle about promotional advertising, especially when grabbing the attention of motorists whizzing by at 50 mph. Larger-than-life images of food are everywhere, from Randy's Donuts to the gargantuan hot dog at Tail o' the Pup, oversized derby hats, and the mammoth chicken of Chicken Boy.

Into the Deep

One of the finest aquaria anywhere, Monterey Bay Aquarium was financed by computer pioneer David Packard and features a 90-foot-long re-creation of Monterey Bay; the tanks are maintained with 1,500 gallons of fresh seawater per minute. Don't miss the three-story kelp forest and the sea otter exhibit.

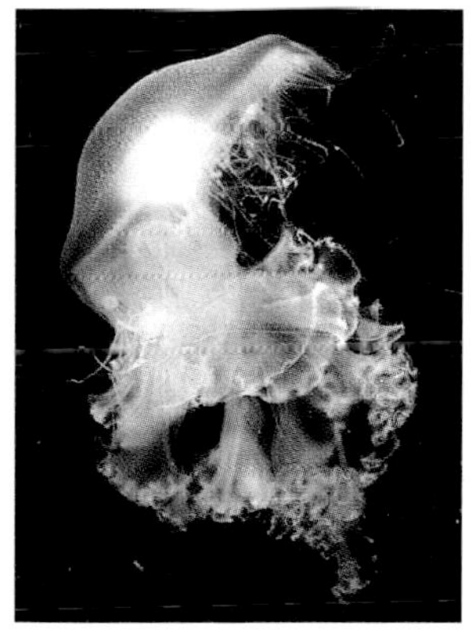

Frederick's of Hollywood Lingerie Museum

The naughty-undies store opened in 1947, followed by the museum. There you'll find historic corsets, bras, and panties donated by stars and starlets from Lana Turner to Belinda Carlisle. On Hollywood Boulevard, it's open during store hours.

Great People

A selective listing of native Californians, concentrating on the arts.

Jack London (1876–1916), adventurer and novelist: *Call of the Wild, White Fang,* and others

Ansel Adams (1902–1984), photographer, environmentalist, inventor of Zone System

Robert Arneson (1930–1992), sculptor

David Belasco (1853–1931), playwright and producer, mentor of Cecil B. DeMille

Elmer Bischoff (1916–1991), painter, leader of Bay Area Figurative Painters

Shirley Temple Black (b. 1928), child movie star and diplomat

Edmund G. (Jerry) Brown (b. 1938), visionary and controversial governor

Joan Brown (1938–1990), painter

John Cage (1912–1992), composer

Henry Cowell (1897–1965), composer

Joan Didion (b. 1934), writer, *Play It As It Lays, The White Album*

Isadora Duncan (1878–1927), dancer and founder of modern choreography

Clint Eastwood (b. 1930), actor and director; mayor of Carmel in late 1980s

William Randolph Hearst (1863–1951), newspaper publisher, entertained le tout Hollywood at Hearst Castle, fictionalized on film as *Citizen Kane*

Steve Jobs (b. 1955) and **Stephen Wozniak** (b. 1951), PC pioneers and founders of Apple Computer

Maxine Hong Kingston (b. 1940), writer known for *China Men*

Ursula LeGuin (b. 1929), science-fiction novelist and poet

George Lucas (b. 1944), film director and producer

Ross Macdonald (1915–1983), creator of the Lew Archer detective novels

Marilyn Monroe (1926–1962), actress and sex symbol

Julia Morgan (1872–1957), architect of "Hearst Castle" and many other buildings

Walter Mosley (b. 1952), author of the Easy Rawlins mysteries

Richard Nixon (1913–1996), U.S. Senator and President

Guy Rose (1867–1925), first California-born artist to win international fame

William Saroyan (1908–1981), novelist, playwright, and short-story writer

Richard Serra (b. 1939), sculptor

John Steinbeck (1902–1968), writer, winner of Pulitzer and Nobel prizes for literature

Amy Tan (b. 1952), novelist, author of *The Joy Luck Club*

Earl Warren (1891–1974), state attorney general and governor, Supreme Court chief justice

. . . and Great Places

Some interesting derivations of California place names.

Alcatraz Spanish for "pelican."

Asilomar Spanish for "sea refuge," now a Monterey conference center.

Anaheim The Germans who settled this Orange County colony in 1858 named it after the Santa Ana River, adding the German suffix *-heim* (home).

Beverly Hills Named for his hometown, Beverly, Mass., by founder Burton Green.

Big Sur An English/Spanish hybrid meaning "big south."

Calistoga Tycoon Sam Brannan developed this mineral springs town as a resort, saying he would make it "the Saratoga of California"; what came out was "the Calistoga of Sarafornia."

Coalinga Known as "Coaling Station" in 1888, it got its present name when a Southern Pacific official added an "a" to "coaling."

Donner A lake, pass, and peak, all named for the ill-fated party of emigrants that attempted to cross the Sierra in the fierce winter of 1846-47.

Fiddletown A mining camp said to have been settled by Missouri miners addicted to fiddling.

Gualala Spanish transliteration of "Valhalla." The coastal hamlet apparently made a romantic impression on early visitors.

Hercules This Solano County town got its name from the local Hercules Powder Company, which made dynamite and rosin.

Malibu The Los Angeles County beach and movie colony gets its name from "Umalibo," a Chumash rancheria.

Modesto William Ralston, a Central Pacific director, declined to have his name applied to the station in 1870. So the Spanish adjective for "modest" was used.

Ophir Only survivor of five mining towns named after the biblical land of gold.

Pomona Named for the Roman goddess of orchards, this Los Angeles County town was famed for its citrus groves.

Rough and Ready A Gold Rush camp in Nevada County given the nickname of General (later President) Zachary Taylor.

San Quentin State penitentiary named not for a saint but for an Indian renegade named Quintin, captured here in 1824.

Sonoma Wintun for "nose"; perhaps after a big-nosed chief.

Tarzana This San Fernando Valley town honors Edgar Rice Burroughs, who lived there while writing his Tarzan adventures.

Yosemite Miwok for "grizzly bear" *(uzumati)*.

Yreka From the indigenous name for Mount Shasta, *Wai-i-ka*.

Sequoia The tree and national park were named for Sequoyah, creator of the Cherokee alphabet.

CALIFORNIA BY THE SEASONS

A Perennial Calendar of Events and Festivals

Here is a selective listing of events that take place each year in the months noted; we suggest calling ahead to local chambers of commerce for dates and details.

January

Mt. Shasta
Alpenfest
Two weekends of dogsled races, ice sculpture contests, teddy bear parade, and "yodel-off."

Pacific Grove
Monarch butterfly migration

Pasadena
Tournament of Roses
The queen of parades, on New Year's Day since 1890.

February

Crescent City
World Championship Crab Races

Indio
Date Festival

Los Angeles and San Francisco
Chinese New Year celebrations

Ripon
Almond Blossom Festival
Marking California's largest tree crop, the event features orchard tours, bake-off, and crowning of Miss Almond Blossom.

March

Los Angeles
Blessing of the Animals
Traditional Mexican event held in Olvera Street, near the city's original plaza.

Mission San Juan Capistrano
Return of the swallows

Oroville
Old-Time Fiddlers' Contest

San Bernardino
National Orange Show

April

Hemet
Ramona Pageant

San Francisco
Japantown Cherry Blossom Festival

San Francisco International Film Festival
Oldest event of its kind in the U.S.; screenings at many venues.

Los Angeles
Los Angeles Bach Festival

May

Angels Camp
Jumping Frog Jubilee/ Calaveras County Fair
The event made famous by the Twain story; frogless enthusiasts can rent an amphibian.

Columbia
Firemen's Muster
Annual event in historic Gold Rush town.

San Diego and Los Angeles
Cinco de Mayo festivals

Monterey
Concours d'Elegance
Fabulous vintage autos (and owners) gather for a vehicular beauty pageant.

San Francisco
Bay to Breakers footrace
10K event draws world-class racers but best known for outlandishly costumed runners.

June

Lompoc
Flower Festival
Acres of this coastal valley are in full bloom. Parade, flower show, entertainment.

Los Angeles and San Francisco
Lesbian and Gay Pride parades

San Juan Bautista
Fiesta
The town boasts one of the the state's oldest missions and was a location for Hitchcock's *Vertigo.*

Modesto
Graffiti U.S.A.
Street fair with '50s music, car show, and "Classic Car Cruz"; a legacy of the George Lucas film.

July

Aptos
World's Shortest Fourth of July Parade

Carmel
Bach Festival

Folsom
Championship Rodeo
One of the state's largest; the other is in Salinas.

Gilroy
Garlic Festival
Famed event in town where Will Rogers said, "you can marinate a steak by hanging it on the clothesline."

Laguna Beach
Festival of the Arts
"Pageant of the Masters" recreates classic and contemporary artworks as *tableaux vivants*.

Orinda
California Shakespeare Festival
Through September.

Redondo Beach
International Surf Festival

San Francisco
Stern Grove Festival
Classical music, dance, theater, jazz, and special events; through August.

Santa Barbara
Old Spanish Days Fiesta

Sonoma
Salute to the Arts
Fine cuisine, wines, music, visual arts, and theater.

Squaw Valley
Tahoe Fat-Tire Festival
Mountain bike races.

August

Cotati
Accordion Festival

Los Angeles
Nisei Week
Celebration throughout Little Tokyo of the city's Japanese-American community.

Sacramento
California State Fair

Salinas
Steinbeck Festival

San Francisco
Comedy Celebration Day
In Golden Gate Park; where some famous stand-ups like Robin Williams got started.

Santa Cruz
Shakespeare Santa Cruz
Festival runs July through early September.

Sausalito
Sausalito Art Festival
Among the biggest juried art and craft shows, since 1952.

Sebastopol
Gravenstein Apple Fair
Arts, crafts, and products made from the early-ripening local apple variety.

September

Crescent City
Seafood Festival

Monterey
Monterey Jazz Festival

Pomona
Los Angeles County Fair
The biggest county fair in the U.S.

October

Half Moon Bay
Art and Pumpkin Festival
Features prize-winning locally grown pumpkins and out-of-state entries.

Pismo Beach
Clam Festival
Celebration of the namesake mollusk of this central coast town of 7,700.

Salinas
California International Air Show

San Francisco
Grand National Rodeo
Blessing of the Fishing Fleet

November

Pasadena
Doo-Dah Parade
Lively spoof features Briefcase Drill Team, Chronic Fatigue Sleepwalkers, and more.

Hollywood
Christmas Parade
Held annually in late November.

December

Carmel
Weihnachtsmarkt
Celebration of the Feast Day of St. Nicholas.

Pescadero
Elephant seal mating season, Año Nuevo State Reserve

WHERE TO GO

Museums, Attractions, Gardens, and Other Arts Resources

Call for seasons and hours when open.

Museums

Ansel Adams Center for Photography
250 4th St., San Francisco, 415-495-7000
Ongoing displays of work by Ansel Adams; changing exhibits of contemporary and historical photography.

Asian Art Museum
Golden Gate Park, San Francisco, 415-668-8921
Jades, bronzes, ceramics, paintings, and other objects from all periods and regions of Asian art.

Behring Auto Museum
3750 Blackhawk Plaza Circle, Danville, 510-736-2277
Collection of unusual autos includes rare Bugattis and Clark Gable's 1935 Duesenberg.

Berkeley Art Museum
Bancroft Way near College Ave., Berkeley, 510-642-1207
Focuses on contemporary and Asian art; formerly known as University Art Museum.

California Academy of Sciences
Golden Gate Park, San Francisco, 415-750-7145
Includes Morrison Planetarium, National History Museum, and the Steinhart Aquarium with its 100,000-gallon Fish Roundabout.

California Afro-American Museum
600 State Drive, Los Angeles, 213-744-7432
Fine arts and history exhibits on African-American life.

California Museum of Science and Industry
700 State Drive, Los Angeles, 213-744-7400
Hands-on exhibits on mathematics, environment, health, earthquakes, and space; five-story IMAX theater.

California Palace of the Legion of Honor
Lincoln Park, 34th and Clement, San Francisco, 415-863-3330
Renaissance through contemporary paintings, prints, and sculpture; striking Beaux Arts building.

California State Railroad Museum
2nd and I Sts., Sacramento, 916-445-4209
Strikingly designed building houses 21 restored locomotives and train cars; also interpretive exhibits, dioramas, and films.

Crocker Art Museum
216 O St., Sacramento, 916-264-5423
Bonanza-era mansion exhibits paintings, drawings, and sculpture by Northern California and European artists.

M. H. DeYoung Memorial Museum
Golden Gate Park, San Francisco, 415-863-3330
Features American art from Colonial period through 20th century; also ancient and ethnographic arts.

Gene Autry Western Heritage Museum
4700 Western Heritage Way, Los Angeles, 213-667-2000
Exhibits showcase the real and mythical history of the American West; vast collection of Western movie memorabilia.

J. Paul Getty Museum
17985 Pacific Coast Highway, Malibu, 310-458-2003
Faithful re-creation of an ancient Roman villa houses collections of antiquities, European paintings, and American and European photographs.

Japanese American National Museum
1st and Central Sts., Los Angeles, 213-625-0414
Exhibits about Japanese emigration to and assimilation into America; occupies a remodeled Buddhist temple.

Los Angeles Children's Museum

310 Main St., Los Angeles, 213-687-8800

Interactive exhibits include TV studio, recording studio, and city streets.

Los Angeles County Museum of Art

5905 Wilshire Blvd., Los Angeles, 213-857-6000

Major regional museum housed in several buildings around a central court; features include permanent collection of paintings, sculpture, costumes, and other arts, Pavilion for Japanese Art, Bing Center theater, two sculpture gardens.

Judah L. Magnes Museum

2911 Russell St., Berkeley, 510-549-6950

"Jewish Museum of the West" offers changing exhibits on Jewish themes; closed Saturdays.

Mexican Museum

Fort Mason, San Francisco, 415-441-1445

First institution of its kind devoted to the arts and culture of Mexico.

Museum of Contemporary Art

250 S. Grand Ave., Los Angeles, 213-626-6222

International works from the 1940s to the present.

Museum of Tolerance

9786 W. Pico Blvd., Los Angeles, 310-553-8403

Interactive exhibits on racism and prejudice in America; major installation on the Holocaust.

Natural History Museum of Los Angeles County

900 Exposition Blvd., Los Angeles, 213-744-3466

Detailed global animal habitats; hands-on children's exhibits; insect zoo; Hall of Native American Cultures.

Norton Simon Museum

411 W. Colorado Blvd., Pasadena, 818-449-6840

Art from the early Renaissance through mid-20th century.

Oakland Museum

10th and Oak Sts., Oakland, 510-834-2413

Dedicated to the art, history, and ecology of California.

George C. Page Museum of La Brea Discoveries

5801 Wilshire Blvd., Los Angeles, 213-936-2230

Reconstructed fossils of ice-age animals found in tar pits; film about prehistoric life in southern California.

Palm Springs Desert Museum

101 Museum Drive, Palm Springs, 619-325-0189

Features Western and contemporary art and Coachella Valley history.

San Diego Museum of Man

Balboa Park, San Diego, 619-239-2001

Features the native cultures of the Americas and ancient Egypt; one of the many museums in Balboa Park to which a single "passport" provides admission.

San Francisco Museum of Modern Art

151 3rd St., San Francisco, 415-357-4000

Spectacular building, opened in 1995, houses permanent collection and international-level changing exhibits.

Southwest Museum

234 Museum Drive, Los Angeles, 213-221-2164

City's oldest museum, in a 1914 Mission Revival building, showcases renowned Native American collections.

Surfing Museum

West Cliff Drive, Santa Cruz, 408-425-7278

Housed in a lighthouse, displays surfabilia from the 1930s to the present.

Tech Museum of Innovation

145 W. San Carlos, San Jose, 408-279-7150

Science and technology exhibits, with an emphasis on computers and high-tech: the development of Silicon Valley, interactive media lab, "digital playroom."

Attractions

ALCATRAZ ISLAND

San Francisco Bay, 415-546-2628

Guided tours of the infamous federal prison, now part of the Golden Gate National Recreation Area.

BERKELEY MUNICIPAL ROSE GARDEN

Euclid Ave. at Bayview Place, Berkeley, 510-644-6530

More than 4,000 varieties of roses in a terraced setting with bay view.

CABLE CAR MUSEUM

Washington and Mason Sts., San Francisco, 415-474-1887

Models, photographs, and relics include the first cable car (1873).

COLUMBIA STATE HISTORIC PARK

Tuolumne County

The entire town is a living museum, with a restored schoolhouse, saloons, and a gold mine tour. The City Hotel serves the best dinner in the Gold Country.

DISNEYLAND

1313 Harbor Blvd., Anaheim, 714-999-4565

"The happiest place on earth"? You be the judge.

EXPLORATORIUM

Bay and Lyon Sts., San Francisco, 415-561-0360

More than 600 interactive exhibits exploring science, math, and technology.

LAWRENCE HALL OF SCIENCE

Centennial Drive, Berkeley, 510-642-5132

Public science center with many hands-on exhibits and a planetarium.

MANN'S CHINESE THEATER

6925 Hollywood Blvd., Los Angeles, 213-461-9624

Hollywood's green-roofed pagoda is a shrine to moviedom, with its cement forecourt bearing the handprints of stars.

MISSION SAN JUAN BAUTISTA

407-623-4528

If you can see only one mission, this is the one: the largest in the chain, it has period furnishings and is still an active Catholic church. Featured in the Hitchcock film Vertigo.

MONTEREY BAY AQUARIUM

886 Cannery Row, Monterey, 408-648-4888

One of the largest aquaria in the world; includes a 90-foot-long re-creation of Monterey Bay, a hands-on tidepool, and a shorebird aviary.

QUEEN MARY

Pier J, Long Beach, 310-435-3511

One of the largest passenger liners ever built, permanently moored in Long Beach Harbor.

SAN DIEGO ZOO

Balboa Park, San Diego, 619-234-3153

More than 4,000 animals of 900 species in lifelike habitats; beautiful landscaping, moving sidewalk, and aerial tram.

UNIVERSAL STUDIOS

Hollywood Fwy. at Lankershim Blvd., University City, 818-508-9600

Tours, special-effects demonstrations, and rides.

WARNER BROS. STUDIOS

Hollywood Way and Olive Ave., Burbank, 818-954-1669

"VIP" walking tour of the studio, including recording stages and prop shops.

Homes and Gardens

LUTHER BURBANK MEMORIAL GARDEN

Santa Rosa and Sonoma Aves., Santa Rosa, 707-576-5115

Displays many plants introduced by the pioneering hybridizer, including the "paradox walnut," Shasta daisy, and spineless cactus.

Descanso Gardens

1418 Descanso Drive, La Cañada, 818-790-7751

A forest of 100,000 camellias surrounding a 30-acre grove of native coast live oaks; spring bulb displays.

Dunsmuir House & Gardens Historic Estate

2960 Peralta Oaks Court, Oakland, 510-615-5555

Forty-acre estate built in 1899 now owned by the City of Oakland; interpretive tours and outdoor concert site.

Filoli

Cañada Road, Woodside, 415-364-2880

Early-20th-century estate with 16 acres of formal gardens.

The Gamble House

4 Westmoreland Place, Pasadena, 818-793-3334

"Ultimate bungalow" by architects Greene & Greene, built in 1908, features hand-shaped beams and original furnishings.

Hearst Castle

Highway 1, north of Cambria, San Simeon, 805 927-2020

Fabulous architecture (by Julia Morgan) and gardens — including nearly 100,000 trees brought to the site.

Hollyhock House

4808 Hollywood Blvd., Los Angeles, 213-662-7272

Frank Lloyd Wright's first building in Los Angeles is a stucco house on a grand scale, with his famous "hidden" entrances.

Huntington Botanical Gardens

1151 Oxford Road, San Marino, 818-405-2141

A wide variety of plantings and garden styles—some 14,000 cultivars on 130 acres, plus an unusual indoor desert garden. Save time for touring the library and museum.

Jack London State Historic Park

One mile west on London Ranch Road, Glen Ellen, 707-938-5216

The author's ranch, home, and grave; also the charred ruins of Wolf House, built but never lived in.

John Muir National Historic Site

4202 Alhambra Ave., Martinez, 510-228-8860

The 17-room residence (built 1882) of the renowned conservationist and author; also the 2-story 1848 adobe in which Muir's daughter lived.

Overfelt Gardens

Educational Park Way off McKee Road, San Jose, 408-251-3323

Botanical garden, Chinese cultural garden, and bird and wildlife sanctuary.

Roses of Yesterday and Today

802 Brown's Valley Road, Watsonville, 408-724-3537

Mail-order nursery and demonstration garden planted with old, rare, unusual, and selected modern roses.

Sunset Magazine Headquarters

Willow and Middlefield Rds., Menlo Park, 415-321-3600

Gardens form a botanical tour of the Pacific Coast, from Pacific Northwest to California desert.

University of California Botanical Garden

Strawberry Canyon off Centennial Drive, Berkeley, 510-642-3343

Plants from every habitat in the world, beautifully landscaped and impeccably labeled.

Other Resources

State Capitol

10th, 15th, L, and N Sts., Sacramento, 916-324-0333

Built 1860–71 and features a 210-foot-high dome.

State Library

914 Capitol Mall, Sacramento, 916-654-0261

California history murals in the general reading room; excellent newspaper and genealogy collections.

CREDITS

The authors have made every effort to reach copyright holders of text and owners of illustrations, and wish to thank those individuals and institutions that permitted the reprinting of text or the reproduction of works from their collections. Those credits not listed in the captions are provided below. References are to page numbers; the designations *a, b,* and *c* indicate position of illustrations on pages.

Text

Aiken & Stone Ltd.: *Journey to Nowhere: A New World Tragedy* by Shiva Naipaul. Copyright © 1986 The Estate of Shiva Naipaul.

American Institute of Wine & Food: "The Farm–Restaurant Connection" by Alice Waters, in *The Journal of Gastronomy*, vol. 5, no. 2 (summer/autumn 1989). Reprinted by permission of the American Institute of Wine & Food.

Farrar, Straus & Giroux, Inc: Ecxerpt from *Play It As It Lays* by Joan Didion. Copyright © 1970 by Joan Didion. Excerpt from *The Kandy-Kolored Tangerine-Flaked Streamline Baby* by Tom Wolfe. Copyright © 1964 and copyright renewed © 1993 by Tom Wolfe. Reprinted by permission of Farrar, Straus, & Giroux, Inc.

Henry Holt and Company: From *The Mohave: A Portrait of the Definitive American Desert* by David Darlington; © 1996 by David Darlington. Reprinted by permission of Henry Holt and Company, Inc.

Houghton Mifflin Company: Excerpt from "Red Wind," from *The Simple Art of Murder* by Raymond Chandler. Copyright 1950 by Raymond Chandler, © renewed 1978 by Helga Greene. Reprinted by permission of Houghton Mifflin Co.

Liveright Publishing Corporation: *My Life* by Isadora Duncan. Copyright 1927 by Boni & Liveright. Renewed © 1955 by Liveright.

New Directions Publishing Corp.: *Miss Lonelyhearts & Day of the Locust,* by Nathanael West. Copyright © 1939 by Estate of Nathanael West. Reprinted by permission of New Directions Publishing Corp.

Oxford University Press: *Inventing the Dream: California Through the Progressive Era* by Kevin Starr. Copyright © 1985 by Oxford University Press, Inc.

Penguin USA, Inc: *Cannery Row* by John Steinbeck. Copyright 1945 by John Steinbeck. Renewed © 1973 by Elaine Steinbeck, John Steinbeck IV and Thom Steinbeck. Used by permission of Viking Penguin, a division of Penguin Books USA Inc.

Random House, Inc.: Lines from "Continent's End" and excerpt from the Introduction, in *The Selected Poetry of Robinson Jeffers.* Copyright 1924 by Peter G. Boyle. Renewed © 1959 by Robinson Jeffers. *The Haight-Ashbury: A History* by Charles Perry. Copyright © 1984 by Rolling Stone Press.

John H. Quinn: *Ishi in Two Worlds: A Biography of the Last Wild Indian in North America* by Theodora Kroeber. Copyright © 1961 by Theodora Kroeber. © renewed 1989 John H. Quinn.

University of Nebraska Press: *California: Land of New Beginnings* by David Lavender. Copyright © 1972 by David Lavender. Reprinted with permission by University of Nebraska Press.

Illustrations

American Craft Museum: **77a** *Couch and Chair with Landscape and Cows* by Richard Shaw, 1966–67. Earthenware, acrylic, and wood. Couch 10 x 18¾ x 9". Chair 9¼ x 9¼ x 9¼". Gift of Johnson Wax Company. Photo Eva Iteyd; Anaheim Public Library: **9** *Spring Eternal* by Langdon Smith, c. 1920; Ansel Adams Publishing Rights Trust: **19** *Mount Williamson* by Ansel Adams, 1945; Gene Anthony: **77b**; The Estate of Robert Arneson: **103b** *California Artist* by Robert Arneson, 1983. Bronze. A.P. 78 x 26 x 22". Photo M. Lee Fatherree; Autry Museum of Western Heritage: **58** Stagecoach, c. 1850s; **92a** *The Banjo Player* by Maynard Dixon, 1901. Pencil, ink, and crayon on paper. 19¼ x 17¼"; Bancroft Library: **14a** Ina Coolbrith; **22a** John Muir; **30a** Yokut hunters; **34a** Map; **35b** Plate; **36a** Taking of Monterey; **38a** Forty-Niner; **41b** Mark Hopkins; **53**; **86a** Bret Harte; **87a, b**; **89a** Joan Didion; Ron Borst/Hollywood Movie Posters: **83b** Brando; **85a** *Beach Party;* **97b** Buster Keaton; **99a** *Hondo;* Braunstein/Quay Gallery: **107** *American Buddha* by Arthur Okamura, 1994. Acrylic on canvas. 68 x 47½"; The Buck Collection: **42** *Ranch Near San Luis Obispo, Evening Light* by Phil Paradise, 1935. Oil on canvas. 28 x 34"; **70** *Ladies in the Garden* by Arthur F. Mathews, 1923. Oil on canvas. 52 x 48"; California Academy of Sciences: **12c** Gold nugget; California Historical Society, San Francisco: **29** Artist in ruins. FN-29921; **41a** Hopkins residence. FN-19296; **43** Rice fields, Stanislaus County. FN-30672; **44a** Crate label. North Baker Research Library. Kemble Collection. Lehmann Label Collection; **55c** Richard Nixon. FN-30673; **62b** Bay Bridge. Photo Rovere Scott. FN-30423; CALIFORNIA STATE AUTOMOBILE ASSOCIATION: **82a**; CALIFORNIA STATE LIBRARY, SACRAMENTO: **15c** Bear flag. California History Room; **31a** Pomo basketweaver. Neg. 3303; **52a** Joshua Norton. Photo Nikki Pahl; CALIFORNIA STATE RAILROAD MUSEUM LIBRARY: **59**; CAMPBELL-THIEBAUD GALLERY: **57** *Freeway Interchange* by Wayne Thiebaud, 1982. Oil on canvas. 30 x 24"; CHIP CLARKE: **109a** Saber-tooth skeleton; WILLIAM CLAXTON: **93b** Jazz cover; THE CONDÉ NAST PUBLICATIONS INC.: **17b** Pulp weekly cover, *Nick Carter's Earthquake Clue*, CORBIS MEDIA: **67a** *Hollywood Jazz* mural; PAUL DAVIS STUDIO: **54c** Huelga poster; DES MOINES ART CENTER: *101 Ocean Park No. 70* by Richard Diebenkorn, 1974. Oil on canvas. 93 x 81". Purchased with funds from the Coffin Fine Arts Trust; Nathan Emory Coffin. 1975.21. Photo Michael Tropea; WALT DISNEY IMAGINEERING: **99b** Photo Peter Aaron/Esto; THE DOCTOR HUEY P. NEWTON FOUNDATION: **55a**; FAMILY DOG PRODUCTIONS: **94a** *Grateful Dead at the Avalon Ball* by Stanley Mouse, 1966. Family Dog is the DBA of Chester Helms, 771 Bush Street, San Francisco, CA 94117; DAVID FECHHEIMER: **88a** *City* magazine cover; FERRY-MORSE SEED COMPANY: **44b** Poster, c. 1898; FINE ARTS MUSEUMS OF SAN FRANCISCO: **20** *Harvest Time* by William Hahn, 1875. Oil on canvas. 36 x 70". Gift of Mrs. Harold R. McKinnon and Mrs. Harry L. Brown. 1962.21; BARBARA GERLACH: **18a** California poppy, Lancaster County; GILCREASE MUSEUM, TULSA: **58a** *Snow Sheds on the Central Pacific Railroad in the Sierra Nevada Mountains* by Joseph Becker, c. 1870. Oil on canvas. 19 x 26"; DAVID LANCE GOINES: **46a** Chez Panisse poster; JIM HEIMANN: **98a** Postcard; **108b** Palomar decal; HERMAN MILLER, INC.: **75a** Chaise. Photo Nick Merrick © Hedrich Blessing; HIRSCHL & ADLER GALLERIES, NEW YORK: **28a** *San Francisco Fire* by William A. Coulter, 1906. Oil on canvas. 60 x 120½"; HISTORY COLLECTIONS, LOS ANGELES COUNTY MUSEUM OF NATURAL HISTORY: **37b** Branding iron. 44½ x 9 x 4"; DAVID HOCKNEY: **102** *Terrace, Hollywood Hills House with Banana Tree*, 1982. Gouache on paper. 51 x 65". Courtesy the artist; ROBERT HOLMES: **108a** Watts Towers, **108c** Paramount Theater, **109b** Randy's Donuts; THE IRVINE MUSEUM: **27** *Point Lobos* by Guy Rose. Oil on canvas. 24 x 29". KENJI TAKI GALLERY: **7b** *Jabo* by Peter Voulkos, 1994. Stoneware stack. 42 x 29 x 26". Photo Hiromu Narita; KATHRYN KLEINMAN: **46b** Salad; COLLECTION GARY KOEPPEL: **88b** *Untitled* (Self-portrait) by Henry Miller, 1962. Watercolor; KOPLIN GALLERY, SANTA MONICA: **5** *Stairway* by James Doolin, 1991–92. Oil on canvas. 90 x 72"; PAUL KRATTER: **26b** *California Sea Otter*, 1997; FRANK LAPENA: **33a** *Flower Dance Spirit*, 1981. Acrylic. 40 x 30". Courtesy the artist; BRUCE LAURITZEN: **106a** *Running Fence;* LEVI STRAUSS & CO: **41c** Levi's label; JOHN LEWIS GLASS STUDIO: **104a** *Glacier Vessel* by John Lewis, 1997. Gold leaf and cast glass. 16 x 11 x 7"; COLLECTION ISAK LINDENAUER: **72a** Lamp. Hammered brass and brass tubing with black abalone-shell shades. 20 x 15½ x 15½"; LOS ANGELES PUBLIC LIBRARY: **64a** Murals. Security Pacific Collection; MERCED COUNTY COURTHOUSE MUSEUM ARCHIVES: **16** *Moraga at the Merced River* by Dorothy Puccinelli, c. 1930s. WPA mural; RICHARD MISRACH: **24** *Palm Tree, California*, 1975. Split-toned gelatin print. Courtesy the artist; MODERNISM INC., SAN FRANCISCO: **104b** *Denny's Arco* by Stephen Hopkins, 1987. Oil with alkyd medium on linen. 71½ x 32½"; MONTEREY BAY AQUARIUM: **109c** Egg-yolk jelly, Outer Bay galleries. Photo D. Wrobel; THE MONTEREY MUSEUM OF ART: **49** *Men of the Sea* by Armin C. Hansen, 1920. Oil on canvas. 51 x 57". Gift of Jane and Dustin Dart. 91.202; MURALISTS OF THE WOMEN'S BUILDING: **67b** *Maestrapiece;* MUSEUM OF THE CITY OF NEW YORK: **40a** Lola Montez. The Harry T. Peters Collection; NATIONAL GEOGRAPHIC SOCIETY IMAGE COLLECTION: **12a** California flag, illustration by Marilyn Dye Smith; **12b** Quail and poppy, illustration by Robert E. Hynes; NATIONAL MUSEUM OF AMERICAN ART/ ART RESOURCE: **39** *Miners in the Sierras* by Charles Christian Nahl with Frederick A. Wenderoth, 1851–52. Oil on canvas. 54¼ x 67". Gift of the Fred Heilbron Collection. 1982.120; NATIONAL PARK SERVICE: **13b** Coast redwood; STATE CAPITOL BOOKSTORE: **13c** State seal; NELSON-ATKINS MUSEUM OF ART, KANSAS CITY, MISSOURI: **96a** *Hollywood* by Thomas Hart Benton, 1937. Tempera with oil on canvas mounted on panel. 53½ x 81". Bequest of artist. © T. H. Benton and R. P. Benton Testamentary Trusts/Licensed by VAGA, New York, NY; NEW BRITAIN MUSEUM OF AMERICAN ART, CONNECTICUT: **26a** *Seal Rock* by Albert Bierstadt, c. 1872. Oil on canvas. 30 x 44". Alix W. Stanley Fund. Photo Michael Agee; NEW-YORK HISTORICAL SOCIETY: **38b** *112 Days to San Francisco*,

Merchant's Express Line of Clipper Ships, White Swallow. Clipper ship card, n.d. Neg. 46620; THE NEW YORKER: **95b** Illustration © Tim Bower. All rights reserved; NIEBAUM-COPPOLA ESTATE, VINEYARDS AND WINERY, RUTHERFORD, CALIFORNIA: **47b** Winery engraving; NORTH CAROLINA MUSEUM OF ART: **23** *Bridal Veil Falls, Yosemite* by Albert Bierstadt, c. 1871-73. Oil on canvas. 36⅛ x 26⅜". Purchased with funds from the North Carolina Art Society (Robert F. Phifer Bequest) and various donors; THE OAKLAND MUSEUM: **30b** Elk antler purse, n.d.; **34b** Spanish armor; **37a** *Californians Catching Wild Horses with Riata* by Hugo Wilhelm Arthur Nahl, n.d. Oil on canvas mounted on masonite. 19⅝ x 23¾". Kahn Collection. Photo M. Lee Fatherree; **40b** Tea urn, presented to Senator E. P. Baker by San Francisco merchants; **50a** Tambourine; **61** *Tower of the Sun* by Chesley Bonestell, 1939; **72b** Desk by Arthur Mathews and Lucia Mathews, The Furniture Shop, 1910–12. Carved and painted wood. 59 x 48 x 20". Gift of Margaret R. Kleinhaus. Photo M. Lee Fatherree; OAKLAND PUBLIC LIBRARY: **15a** Sheet music; OLD GLOBE THEATRE: **91c** Falstaff; ORANGE COUNTY MUSEUM OF ART: **18b** *Silver and Gold* by Granville Redmond, c. 1918. Oil on canvas. 30 x 40". Gift of Mr. and Mrs. J. G. Redmond; PALM SPRINGS DESERT MUSEUM: **103a** *After the Alcatraz Swim #3* by Joan Brown, 1976. Gift of Steve Chase in honor of the 10th anniversery of the Contemporary Art Council. DM 14-94. Photo Avra-Waggaman; PHOEBE A. HEARST MUSEUM OF ANTHROPOLOGY, UNIVERSITY OF CALIFORNIA AT BERKELEY: **33a** Ishi shaping bow with adze; PHOTOFEST: **96b** Gloria Swanson; **97a** *The Maltese Falcon;* PHOTO RESEARCHERS: **15b** Butterfly; PILKINGTON-OLSOFF FINE ARTS, INC.: **81a** *Chinese New Year Parade,* 1992. Acrylic on linen. 84 x 120½". PRIVATE COLLECTION: **51b** *Star Gazer* by Agnes Pelton, 1929. Oil on canvas. 30 x 16". Photo William A. Karges Fine Art, Los Angeles; THE REAGAN LIBRARY: **55b** Button; FRANK ROMERO: **82b** *Downtown,* 1990. Courtesy the artist; ED RUSCHA: *100 Trademark 3,* 1962. Mixed media on paper. 9½ x 14½". Courtesy the artist; SAN DIEGO HISTORICAL SOCIETY: **50b** Souvenir album; SAN DIEGO MUSEUM OF MAN: **31b** Paiute basket; SAN FRANCISCO MARITIME MUSEUM: **48a** *The Caspar* by Herman R. Dietz, c. 1890. Oil on canvas. 55 x 90 cm.; SAN FRANCISCO MIME TROUPE: **91a** Photo Mark Estes; SAN FRANCISCO OPERA: **95a**; SAN FRANCISCO PERFORMING ARTS LIBRARY & MUSEUM: **90a, b**; **91b**; **93a** Chinese opera; SANTA BARBARA MISSION ARCHIVE LIBRARY: **35a** *Mission San Gabriel* by Ferdinand Deppe, 1832. Oil on canvas. 27¼ x 36¾"; ANNE SCHECHTER AND REID BUCKLEY: **63** *Victory Shipyards I* by Erle Loran. Photo courtesy Fine Arts Museums of San Francisco; Richard Schloss: **74a** *Clearing Storm, Santa Barbara,* 1995. Oil on canvas. 24 x 36". Courtesy the artist; COLLECTION JERRY SLOVER: **83a** Ford coupe; SUPERSTOCK: **98b** Marilyn Monroe; JOSEPH SZYMANSKI: **21** *Southern Sierras* by Joseph Breuer, 1915. Oil on canvas. 36 x 42"; TROTTER GALLERIES CARMEL, CA: **2** *Cypress Trees—17 Mile Drive* by Mary DeNeale Morgan, c. 1925. Oil on canvas. 20 x 16"; UNDERWOOD PHOTO ARCHIVES, SF: **54a** AP Photo; UNIVERSITY ART MUSEUM, UNIVERSITY OF CALIFORNIA AT BERKELEY: **45** *Still Life and Blossoming Almond Trees (The Stern Mural)* by Diego Rivera, 1931. Fresco. 62¼ x 105"; UNIVERSITY ART MUSEUM, UNIVERSITY OF CALIFORNIA, SANTA BARBARA: **25** *Death Valley, Dante's View* by Fernand Lungren, n.d. Oil on canvas. 26 x 60". Fernand Lungren Bequest; UNIVERSITY OF CALIFORNIA, SANTA CRUZ, SPECIAL COLLECTIONS: **89b** *The one who comes to question himself* by Kenneth Patchen, c. 1966. 42.8 x 27.3 cm.; DAVID WEINGARTEN: **17a** Golden Gate Bridge, c. 1960s. Cast brass miniature. 2½ x 6"; WELLS FARGO BANK HISTORY ROOM: **52b** Engraving, Casey and King; WEST LIGHT: **73** Photo Steve Smith; WINDGATE PRESS: **60a** *Palace of Fine Arts* by Jules Guérin. Hand-tinted photograph; ROBIN WINFIELD: **106b** SFMOMA, 1996. Cibachrome print and acrylic; STEPHEN WIRTZ GALLERY: **105** *Things were never $1.50* by Raymond Saunders, 1995. Mixed media on wood and door. 96 x 83". Photo Charles Frizzell.

Acknowledgments

Walking Stick Press wishes to thank our project staff: Miriam Lewis, Kina Sullivan, Laurie Donaldson, Georgia Finnigan, Daniel Golden, Adam Ling, and Catherine Scott.

For other assistance with *California,* we are especially grateful to: Laurel Anderson/Photosynthesis, Ron Borst/Hollywood Movie Posters, the California Historical Society, Lee Cox at the San Francisco Performing Arts Library & Museum, Robin Dunitz, Brian Gross of Brian Gross Fine Arts, Mary Haas at the Fine Arts Museums of San Francisco, Robert Holmes, Lindsay Kefauver/Visual Resources, Richard Ogar at the Bancroft Library, Carl Ryanan-Brant and Joy Tahan at the Oakland Museum, and the staffs of the San Francisco, Berkeley, and Oakland public libraries.